Praise for *Way Out Here* by Richard Leo

"This is an extraordinary book about how to see. Plant, animal, family, neighbor, and mountain are all equally worthy of attention and love in Leo's view. This perspective creates wholeness. He makes remote Alaska seem connected to every world."

—Gerald Jampolsky, MD
author of *Love Is Letting Go of Fear*

"With a prose style that is witty, surprising, and penetrating, Richard Leo combines anecdote and reflection to convey how the experience of homesteading in Alaska can be a wide window into the human condition. In the best tradition of American nature writing, *Way Out Here* is both profoundly humane and wild. This book will be appreciated because, in the end, it is about all of us and the world we love and yet may save. Leo quickly becomes not only our trusted guide in a shared spiritual encounter with the wildness within and without, but our intimate friend, and we do not want the book to end."

—Professor J. Ronald Engel
Chair of Ethics Working Group of World Conservation Union,
Meadville/Lombard Theological School at the
University of Chicago

MODERN LIFE IN ICE-AGE ALASKA

WAY OUT HERE

RICHARD LEO

SASQUATCH BOOKS
SEATTLE

For Mom

Printed in the United States of America.

Cover and interior design: Julie N. Long
Cover photograph: Mount Brooks, Denali National Park.
 Photograph by Darrell Gulin/Tony Stone Images.
Cover inset photograph: Richard Leo
Composition: Sue D. Cook

Library of Congress Cataloging-in-Publication Data
Leo, Richard.
 Way out here : modern life in ice-age Alaska / Richard Leo.
  p.   cm.
 ISBN 1-57061-061-4
 1. Susitna River Valley (Alaska)—Social life and customs. 2. Susitna River Valley (Alaska)—Description and travel. 3. Leo, Richard—Homes and haunts—Alaska—Susitna River Valley. I. Title.
F912.S95L46   1996
979.8'3—dc20   96-4292

Sasquatch Books
1008 Western Avenue
Seattle, Washington 98104
(206)467-4300

No way out here.

Here is there, waiting.

White swans rise winging.

—Ho-san

ACKNOWLEDGMENTS

Thanks to Ma and Wa and Ca and Willow for loving both me and this world, for believing in their own perceptions.

This book also required the support and advice of David Black, Susan Raihofer, Gary Luke, Frank Robinson, Betty Musser, Dot Fisher-Smith, Mark Haley, John Leo, Marian Wood, the *Anchorage Daily News*, and Mrs. Porter's College Composition class, among others, for which I am grateful.

/\\.\\.\\.\\

Contents

Map   9

Introduction   11

What's Here   13

Around the Homestead   21

Kids in the Woods   71

Community   101

Neighbors   121

The Necessary and Sentient Sled Dog   135

Mountains and Expeditions   149

The Wider View: Change and Continuity   177

Ultimately   189

/\/\/\/\

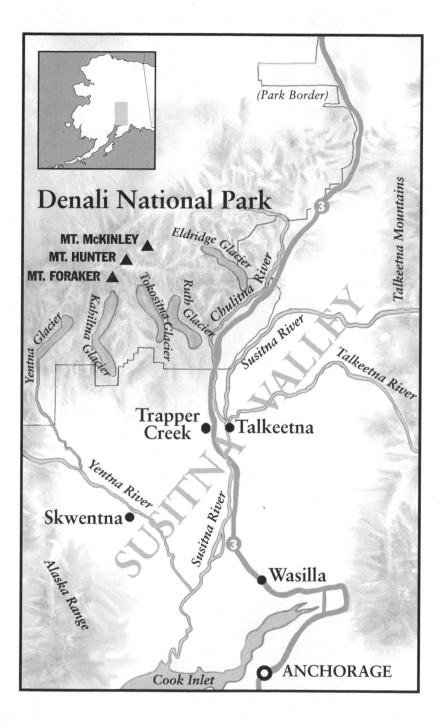

Denali National Park

MT. McKINLEY
MT. HUNTER
MT. FORAKER

Eldridge Glacier

Tokositna Glacier

Ruth Glacier

Chulitna River

Kahiltna Glacier

Yentna Glacier

(Park Border)

Talkeetna Mountains

Susitna River

Talkeetna River

Trapper Creek · · Talkeetna

SUSITNA VALLEY

Yentna River

Skwentna ·

Susitna River

Alaska Range

Wasilla

ANCHORAGE

Cook Inlet

—9—

INTRODUCTION

Nothing in the view from our ridge in Alaska's Susitna Valley has changed in the fifteen years since we first homesteaded deep in the woods. To the north and west the massive jagged bulwark of Denali (Mount McKinley) and its flanking snow peaks rises so abruptly from the forested lowlands that the sky seems pierced. Above the trees to the east blue foothills roll up to the lesser but still glaciated Talkeetna mountains, walling the valley's opposite side. To the south the distant Pacific Ocean builds successive waves of clouds.

To all horizons only forest and mountains and sky are visible. Beyond our small clearing there is no other human sign, no road, no building, no campfire.

The biggest change in this landscape in 5,000 years has been the slow withdrawal of the glaciers farther into the surrounding mountains. More habitat has been created: deeper canyons for bears to den and swans to breed, longer clear-water creeks for salmon to spawn, thicker willow and birch stands where moose browse.

In my own life, however, this sudden evolution has occurred: I no longer think it's possible to escape from *anything*. Living in a remote part of a vast valley doesn't free us from economic worry or planetary pollution or cultural influences or our own selves. No landscape or lifestyle is absolution from that which we carry into it.

And yet because I have widely published depictions of life in wilderness Alaska, I get letters from around the industrial world asking for details about how to "get away" too. There is such longing in these requests, such need to find an alternative to shopping malls and rush-hour traffic and stressful careers and the opiate of television.

This book is not a primer for those desires.

Once I thought I could create an entire culture in this valley hidden for almost all human history by the encompassing snow mountains. My own private Shangri-la, I figured, removed from constant change.

But change, of course, is the only constant of organic life.

Any hope, I know now, for the creation of a good world, a peaceful heart, a whole life has little to do with where it's placed. The answer to desire isn't in wild Alaska, the caves of Tibet, or the penthouse suites of corporate towers. It's in the way we see where we are. It's in what we choose to look at twice, on what we focus our attention.

This book is about the way I see a land that at this moment seems fixed in time: a clear summer sky, winged bugs held like pollen in the amber sunshafts of evening, tall grasses rippling beneath a rolling breeze, mountains on the horizons as brilliant and white as dream. I can see this land as it once was because it still is.

There are also the commensurate realities of long-discussed but as yet latent logging roads and tourist resorts and other "developments" designed to "do something" with the valley.

But in these pages the focus is on what already exists here, and always has—which includes the faith of possibility, great beauty, and grace—in hopes of discovering a way of seeing that can be carried anywhere, to find what matters in any place.

IS THE REAL QUESTION
WHO AM I? OR
WHEN AM I HERE?
— HO-SAN

WHAT'S HERE

In winter, Alaska's Susitna Valley records some of the most severe weather on earth: blizzards approaching 100 degrees below zero near the surrounding glaciated mountains, as much as twenty-five feet of snow on the valley floor.

The twelve feet of snow we average per winter at our homestead requires that we dig a trench to reach the doorway. Winds pack the snow like cement against the north side of the house. Our five-year-old son will commonly wear a face mask and ski goggles to play outside when the windchill bites.

But in summer the same valley is a temperate rain forest. As in any rain forest, the amount of life is staggering. There are constant echoing bird calls, huge dew-slick ferns, swarming bugs, spawning salmon, and wolves. Underbrush is so dense a machete is standard equipment for travel through the overhanging woods.

Nowhere else on earth does such an icescape transform into a humid jungle, seasonally.

Winter's aurora borealis and silverpoint starfields fade behind the constant daylight of sub-arctic summers. For three months bracketing the summer solstice the sky grows no dimmer than a pastel orange radiance during the "night."

The U-shaped valley is enormous. It contains 4,000 square miles of spruce and birch streaked by long open tundra meadows studded with shallow lakes. Few people live amidst its wilds. The great parabola of snow mountains that contains the valley is surmounted by Denali, the continent's tallest peak, the highest vertical rise on earth.

Hundreds of creeks like veins descend through canyons creasing those mountains. They all flow into the Susitna River, which lies in the center of the valley. The Big Su drains America's fifth-largest volume of water relative to its length. Only the Mississippi, the Ohio, the Columbia, and the Yukon are bigger.

Not long ago an ice sheet thousands of feet thick once filled the entire valley. It flowed unimpeded 150 miles south from the valley's top into the Pacific Ocean. That ice remained for most of the 35,000 years during which human beings gradually populated the Western Hemisphere after crossing the wide Bering land bridge from Asia. Those original Americans curved around the valley's insurmountable arc of snow peaks to follow ice-free grasslands into the rest of the truly New World.

Then as now the land beyond the concealed valley was too dry to build glaciers; moisture blown up from the Pacific was caught by the range and dropped inside the valley walls. While Inuit and Clovis and Mayan and Aztec and Inca cultures gradually evolved, this valley was completely hidden from *Homo sapiens.*

Not until as recently as 500 years after Christ did the first people crest the passes between the lowest mountains to gaze down into the valley.

What those fur-clad Athabascan Indians saw must have been staggering.

If the season was early summer—which I assume was the

case, because game trails leading into the passes are evident before the explosion of greenery, and because freedom from snow slog makes wandering joyous—and if the skies were clear, which they commonly are at that time of year, the expanse below probably made them weep at its beauty or laugh abruptly at the unexpected marvel or whoop-'n'-holler with the discovery or simply stand in silent communion with something profound and powerful. An entirely different ecosystem than that from which they'd come stretched before them, the newest arable land on earth.

What they saw was this: an ocean of gold-green birch canopies budding into leaf commingled with the darker green of spruce rising to foothills covered by russet alpine tundra, above which stood white mountains of such height and mass the horizon bent. Curtains of breeding swans and geese rose and fell in the tributary canyons lush with willow and alder and marsh grasses fed by the melting blue ice of the still-withdrawing glaciers.

Even the scent was different from the sparser, more arid land north of the range—richer, more floral, *bigger.* Everything would have seemed bigger. The fecundity was and is unparalleled two latitude degrees below the Arctic Circle.

Now horticulturists in the lower part of the valley grow cabbages the size of sports cars, beets like basketballs, anaconda-thick zucchini. The upper valley grows some of the world's largest salmon and trout, moose and bear.

Anchorage, with 275,000 people, Alaska's largest city, sits on the Pacific coast twenty miles from the tidal delta of the Susitna River, yet is isolated from the valley by a flanking range of coastal mountains, the Chugach. Two hundred-twenty miles from Anchorage by the only road up through the valley, the route to the valley winds over the winnowing end of the Denali massif into the rest of Alaska.

That two-lane blacktop road wasn't completed until the 1970s. Until then access to the reaches of the upper valley, where we live, was as limited as to the roadless areas of Nepal.

Even before the advent of Caucasian exploration and inadvertently introduced disease, the aboriginal population of the valley was not much more than a thousand at its highest. Athabascan seasonally nomadic hunter-gatherer technologies were not conducive to empire building. The land remained impervious to easy travel or permanent settlement: deep snow by winter, dense underbrush by summer.

Real wild land accepts habitation on its own terms.

In 1896 the first American to leave record followed a fever into the valley. He was drawn not by wanderlust nor pilgrimage nor vision quest, but by gold. Explorer and prospector William Dickey—an Ohioan—stood on an alpine tundra pass to look up, and up, at the world's most abrupt mountain. He wrote a dispatch when he returned to "civilization" that the *New York Sun* printed ballyhooing the "discovery" of "Mount McKinley," named for an Ohio politician who championed the gold standard.

The discovery of gold in the foothills of the mountain that the Athabascans called Denali had a much greater impact.

By 1905 the foothills on either side of the valley were being prospected. The miners ventured into the land by boat, dogsled, snowshoe, and donkey. Their numbers peaked at perhaps 3,000 when the Alaska Railroad from the Gulf of Alaska was completed in 1923. Fairbanks, across the range, was the destination and terminus of the railroad, because of the far more extensive gold rush in the Territory of Alaska's interior, north of the Susitna Valley. More than *40,000* people flooded that country.

The railroad also created a small village near the center of the upper valley at the confluence of the Susitna with its two largest secondary rivers. Talkeetna boomed as a railroad construction camp (a clapboard bar-and-inn, a general store, a score of cabins on platted house sites along the mud "Main Street") and then busted when the gold finds didn't amount to anything like those in the Klondike or Nome or Fairbanks.

By the mid-1930s some miners remained in the upper valley, along with the last of Talkeetna's shopkeepers, a few trappers, and the dwindling Athabascan population.

The cumulative effect of this second wave of human incursion into the valley was the same as the original aboriginal migration: the profundity of the wilderness was little affected.

Bears avoided the scattered log cabins of the remaining placer miners toughing it out in the foothills. Ravens flew over trackless forest to cross the blip of Talkeetna amidst the trees. New growth covered trails. Winter buried the land for most of the year.

The valley remained one of the least explored, mapped, and known areas on the planet.

World War II brought a flurry of activity to the Alaska Territory. An army base in the coastal town of Anchorage doubled the population to 10,000. Statehood in 1959 brought another influx of federal money. Still, little in the valley changed. Talkeetna's population remained at a few hundred. Few of the peaks walling the valley had been climbed, most not even named. The railroad ran just a few trains a week on through to Fairbanks, mostly freight. Finally, in 1974 when the Trans-Alaska Oil Pipeline started construction—the next Alaskan boom—change began to reach into the valley. The town of Wasilla, on an arm of the Pacific just twenty air miles north of Anchorage, was incorporated that year, soon becoming the fastest-growing community in America. Wasilla is now the hub of the lower valley, grown to 4,400 industrious people, with a central business strip lined by a McDonald's, a Wendy's, a Burger King, a Taco Bell, a Pizza Hut, two 7-11s, three shopping malls, a mutable number of banks that go boom and bust, and a hundred other small businesses ranging from dogsled supply stores to hairdressing salons. About one third of Wasilla's work force commutes to Anchorage.

North of Wasilla, signs of economic development are increasingly widely spaced along the single road up through the valley: Ivan's Bait and Tackle ("Live Worms"), Goble's Gamble Ar-Vee Dumpsite, Wolf Safari ("You Getta Pettum"). Telephone and powerlines that follow the road stop halfway between Wasilla and the pass out of the valley.

Two of Denali's glaciers, the thirty-six-mile-long Ruth and the thirty-mile-long Eldridge, come to within four miles of the blacktop. The smaller and more distant Peters surged five miles in 1985, 200-foot ice towers toppling in its path.

Official wilderness areas of Denali National Park include most of the high country that defines the north and west arc of the upper valley. Denali State Park is contiguous, extending across the lowland forests to the eastern foothills. All that parkland, too, is wild: almost wholly trailless and uninhabited.

The entire population of the upper valley, by the most recent census, is 920. Half that number is in the riverbank village of Talkeetna. People come and go, build cabins in the woods and then flee the isolation, collect welfare in the village while waiting for a real job elsewhere, buy into a small business and then sell out.

Most of us who remain do so because of what we see in the land. The power and beauty of this place is as necessary to those of us who have chosen it as the Tibetan highlands are to those who originally found sustenance there.

One major difference, however, between historic Tibet and this equivalently remote and mountain-dominated world is that here there are no monks, no people who don't try to fix or improve their economic world. This is, after all, America's Alaska, the culmination of Manifest Destiny where the pioneers are determined to make a "better" life than that which they've left.

The valley remains new to human habitation. Immigrants bring their culture with them. Only in time do they adapt to what is pervasive in the land.

The Susitna Valley is unique not just for its extremes of climate, its contrasts in culture (true wilderness accessible within a three-hour drive of fast food), or its *terra incognita* status in human history. This valley is *familiar*, paradoxically; it resonates deeply in our collective unconscious. Human beings took their last evolutionary step into that which we are today amidst a Pleistocene environment duplicated here: conifer forests rising to game-rich tundra rising to glacial canyons within which cave bears den. Long severe winters and short intense summers. Proximate perennial ice.

When Ice Age glacial sheets covered much of North America, Europe, and Asia, this landscape and climate was what we knew. Our genetic dispositions have a basis here—dispositions to dominate and to herd together for the sake of survival, to wander alone in hope of revelation, instinctively to seek *more* in order to allay fear of scarcity, and to stand silently, if only for a moment, in humility and awe at all that exists beyond ourselves.

A few years ago I spent an afternoon with the (now former) Superintendent of Denali National Park, discussing the park lands within the Susitna Valley. His belief was that the human proclivity to expand our domain ultimately cannot be denied nor contained, nor should it necessarily be. "Because when we've come to the ends of the earth there will still be the stars!"

I tend to believe that the manner in which the earth is reaching the end of its capacity to sustain our proclivities bodes poorly for the stars. The universe may be infinite but our desires are redundant, and "more" is a limited philosophy of life. "Further" will inevitably bring us back to just where we are.

This valley now is a stage on which to see much of human history recapitulated. Here's a lab to study the nature of our nature, perhaps the last and best place for maintaining a connection between what we've been and what we've become, where we have deepest roots and where we've just arrived, that which has always been fundamental and that which seems necessary at the moment.

Last spring I went up to Alder Point, a 4,000-foot foothill flanking the terminus of the Ruth Glacier. It was March, the traveling conditions were good (firm snow, lengthening daylight), the sky was clear, and the hike up the peak was easy after securing the dogteam at its base. The view was so expansive I idled through the dusk. The great mountains above were silhouetted against the last lingering light.

Then with a start I realized that the entire valley below me was dark. There was no visible point of light anywhere—no houselight, no streetlight, no campfire, no nothing.

As more and more stars came out the forested valley floor became blacker and blacker. I knew that fifty miles away was the beacon of the Talkeetna air strip, but it was lost in the expanse.

I saw streaking meteors and the outline of the peaks against the starscape. That was all.

I began to worry that I wouldn't be able to find my camp. The valley, I understood once again, was that vast. I yelled for the dogs but my voice had no echo.

Then, eerily, the dogs far below began to sing with the wavering howl of wolves. When I'd fixed my direction, I started down.

An hour later I stumbled into camp. The dogs wagged their tails.

It was all familiar. It was all unearthly.

AROUND THE HOMESTEAD

Our homestead is not so much the center of our world as it is the base, the jumping-off point. For millennia Western civilization thought of Earth as the center of the universe. The cosmos was considered to be rather like what we knew as home, just bigger. It seems so much more true to see what sustains us as a very small place from which to investigate the endless and utterly unfamiliar Everything Else.

Near the foothills of Denali, far removed from any road, the homestead's main log house, "guest" cabin (read: "place to store stuff"), sauna, root cellar, woodshed, and garden are together smaller than a nice suburban ranch house. But The Ridgeline (as we've come to call our twenty forested acres in the grand manner of baronial estates and trailer parks) feels expansive. Our three boys have to use a whiffle ball to play baseball because any ball more solid will be hit beyond the small clearing and lost in brush. And yet the area in which we bat seems plenty big, like a car-less street would seem for city stickball.

Fifteen years ago, not long arrived from New York City, the 75 spruce I felled from various corners of the land for cabin logs seemed like plunder to me, an excessive impact on the landscape. Now, however, each season we have to whack berry bushes and vines and saplings from the 50-by-25-foot "backyard" just to keep it clear of the continuously encroaching forest.

The spring from which we dip water into buckets for drinking is fifty yards down the ridge; the creek where we fish in summer or ice skate in winter is fifty yards beyond that; the swimming lake is a quarter mile away out on the open tundra. These distances require stepping away from the cleared area into the forest where in truth a grizzly could be passing coincidentally, to grim possibilities. But the sense of connection between those nearby places and the psychological safety of the homestead structures has become intuitive; there's no separation between the uncertain "there" and secure "here."

From that beginning the wider circles of connection expand. By dogsled in good conditions we're about an hour from the mountains; they've moved closer in our conception of what's "part" of the homestead and what isn't. By foot in summer the gravel road where we leave our truck is two hours away, but the trail has become so familiar that it's hard to retain the original mind-set of being "isolated" in the woods.

This awareness of being connected to more of the world than a glimpse of the tiny clearing amidst the trees would indicate means that there's an absence of the feeling of alienation. Anxiety isn't a part of the general mood of daily life. Not anymore. At first, though, there were times of raw terror, waking up suddenly in the middle of the night, heart pounding, to stare through the bedside window and think, "What is *out* there?" Now the land's benign. It's all home.

There are still dangers, of course, and we're a long way from a hospital. My wife's a skilled midwife, with both Western medical training and a practical wisdom about traditional healing arts. But having an in-house doctor doesn't remove the risks inherent in living remote.

Those risks, however, are familiar now, not frightening. It's a practice in attention to deal with good ol' dangers like felling trees or loading a gun or just walking the trail.

And so we can concentrate on what else there is to see.

ᴧᴧᴧ REACHING HOME

After having been anywhere in the wider human world—the post office (a full day's trip there and back) or our closest neighbor's house (across two ridges and a creek)—getting home requires a trek.

In the winter it's a cruise by dogsled. Except during or just after a heavy snow when the dogs have to swim like porpoises (dive, paddle, surface, breathe, dive, paddle, surface, breathe...), the run is fun. It's like downhill skiing on level ground: Knees bent! Keep your balance! *Zoom.*

The few others who live in the roadless part of the valley use a snowmachine to reach their cabins, or cross-country skis.

But in summer there lurks the possibility that the long, unavoidable walk will become an unwelcome chore, a slow, soggy, annoying commute. A backpack (to carry supplies) is as requisite as rubber rain boots, so there's no chance for a smart jog. The trail can get so overgrown with brush that the ground itself is an assumption; a step can be an act of faith.

It's the summer trail, though, that provides necessary perspective, in part because it *isn't* luge-chute adrenaline-amped swift. The length of the hike and the variation in terrain usually forces anything being carried internally to be dropped. All the stuff from having been out in the social world—petty angers, imagined slights, flattering compliments—gets chucked to decrease weight, but not right away.

First comes the recapitulation. The beginning of our trail lends itself to an overview of Life, because it's hard. Sloughs cut channels that need to be leaped, grunting. The creek yearly washes out parts of the path, requiring a stomp through new brush. The fertile flood-deposited soil grows head-high grasses, tangles of willow. Those first few hundred yards create the opportunity to consider what I *really* should have said on the pay phone to the credit collection company, to kick at the brush in my guilt for having been abrupt with a friend who would have liked a patient ear. I stumble across the sloughs and flail at the grasses.

Then the trail crosses a giant cottonwood with a three-foot-thick trunk that for fifteen years has spanned the creek, an absolutely necessary bridge still withstanding flood and rot. It fell, of its own, exactly at the point and during the time when a way was needed across the water. A cottonwood is one of the rare trees that existed during the time of the dinosaurs. I see miracle every time I balance my way over it. Life is suffering, sure, but there is also a whole lot else going on.

For the next few miles the trail meanders through forest, high ground. Walking becomes easier. Sunlight filters through the tree tops. Kinder memories surface. Those carried from the road begin to drop away.

Right beneath this spruce we once found a bird's nest with six small chicks in it. Just over there was where we scared a black bear from a moose carcass. Here is the spot where we discovered a trail-side spring behind the ferns and brought a cup to leave beside it. Mingled with the memories are new perceptions of the day: moose prints, fresh, cow and very young calf; pink blueberry flowers opening a week or two earlier than usual, maybe from the winter's light snowfall, warmer soil; the song of lots of Swainson's thrushes, good, the loveliest melody of all the valley's migratory birds; whoa! that bear scat wasn't there last week. Time to sing my own songs, *loud,* to announce my presence.

"My feets are my only carriage / so I got to push on through..."

Within the hour the trail opens onto a long, narrow stretch of tundra, a moist fairway of ankle-high flowers and grasses. The mountains rise on the revealed horizon. Even if it's cloudy I know they're there, above the stratus.

The walking's harder, though, squishing along. The tundra is a dense mat of vegetation atop ground water. This is where lingering hindsight (...maybe I should have waited for the day's mail to come in, just in case...) becomes foresight: anticipating the end of the trek, hollering hello to the kids, bringing news to my wife, sharing what I've packed in to eat or read. If the dogs are barking, their voices waft in and out on breezes.

Sandhill cranes occasionally feed on the tundra. Once a black bear trailing four (count 'em) cubs crossed the trail on the far side of the biggest lake. That sure provides a quick shift of perspective.

Something always happens, though, even as simple as having a dragonfly light on my shoulder. Everything that occurs takes my attention. It's difficult to remain involved with myself.

Those couple of hours just to get home from anywhere are as essential to this life as the bridge across the creek. Rushing to get *there* misses *here*. Each slow step reveals something new. There is always more than what we first see. Otherwise what we know is all there is, which is terminal.

⋀⋀⋀ SPRING

There are still two feet of snow on the ground though the stars have already been burned from the midnight sky by unending daylight. The snow pack has settled so firmly that it's like greased concrete, making the whole world a highway for sled travel. The birch are beginning to bud and the first of the songbirds have returned.

There are no bugs. Nothing to swat at, wave away, suffer.

Brilliant sun by day. Cold and luminous by night. Mushing in a tee-shirt. Skiing in shorts. And no bugs.

I am goofy with happiness at how perfect this all is. There's no flood and no mud, no slog and no sweat. This is the brief season with the very best of both summer and winter. Fish are biting in the open creek and any animal can be tracked casually by its prints in the snow.

This morning was below freezing, solidifying the snow cover. Two trumpeter swans flew overhead. Suntan time in a few hours on the back porch.

What more from a world could be asked?

This could be asked: is a short period of primo excellence worth months and months of blizzard and drizzle and slop and struggle and bugs?

Christianity has the concept of epiphany: "a sudden appearance or manifestation of God in His glory." Zen calls the same thing *kensho:* a moment, without time reference, in which the divine is present everywhere, ecstatically. Modern psychology, in its endearingly bumbling way, offers terms such as "self-actualization" and "peak experience." The idea is all the same. After travail, *yes.*

Often I find myself complaining about the weather, and then it changes, and I complain about that, and then it changes, and I find something not quite right again until I'm exhausted trying to get the climate to fit my needs.

So here it is: just what I want. Day after day of it, unexpectedly.

When climbers attempt Denali they suffer through weeks of grueling slog until, maybe, they stand on the summit in sun for a few minutes. Is it worth the struggle? Ho!

When serious anglers gear up for the salmon season they can wait to hook into one for what seems like forever, cast after cast, hope after hope after nibble. Then when a big fish finally strikes and the line whizzes out singing, does it eradicate the frustration of having stood inert in the rain?

What about monks endlessly practicing prayers or prostrations in aching expectation of revelation: when the white light and tears descend, has a lifetime been absolved?

There is a whole lot of light on this world now, summit bright. Does it make up for the forty below and the brown fall floods and the bugs? Why, even a single day of this spring idyll is enough to—

Damn. A mosquito just bit me.

/\/\/\

The birds are back. Sandpipers and phalaropes on the tundra. Thrushes and swallows and sparrows and warblers in the woods. The great geese overhead.

The boreal forest is once again wired for sound. Whales and dolphins "see" with their ears deep in the ocean. Their world becomes three-dimensional not with binocular vision but with chirps and trills and songs. Standing in this deep green forest at dawn or dusk is like snorkeling into a humpback whale migration: the sound comes from everywhere.

But now that the birds are back, what are they going to eat? There is still snow general over all the land. The creeks are open, but the lakes remain frozen. How will the flocks survive? This is not bird-feeders-in-every-backyard country, mainly because there are so few backyards.

Once, after a winter hunt, we cut open the gullet of a spruce hen—a grouse, a wild chicken—to see what it ate in January. We found a hundred spruce needles, nothing else. Its intestines smelled like spruce. We stared across the forest at the sea of spruce. Talk about heaven on earth for the right kind of bird.

The black-capped and boreal chickadees that live here through the winter eat the twig ends of birch where the seeds remain. There are almost as many birch as spruce in this part of the forest. What a rich land. If you have the right kind of stomach.

For 140 million years this part of the world was a tropical swamp where dinosaurs had it as easy as spruce grouse and chickadees do now. The large ostrich ferns that will be the first green shoots after the snow melts off were even larger then. But what are the migratory birds going to do for the next few weeks waiting for the ground to thaw or the continents to shift again?

Maybe the geese and swans that are spiralling back to their breeding grounds have some way to feed that isn't apparent to me. Certainly the light radiant on the snow is beautiful, but is spiritual nourishment sufficient to keep them healthy?

I've learned that just a few open leads in otherwise frozen creeks can allow aquatic birds to feed. Old vegetation swirling beneath the current is better than no vegetation. That doesn't seem to answer the needs of 10,000 birds, however. It also fails to address the needs of perching birds and songbirds and robins who won't find worms for weeks.

But here they all are, plainly aware of something that I'm not. From a bird's eye view the land is already greened to the south. Summer's happening down along the coast near Anchorage while this upper valley remains another season. Still, the birds here don't commute a couple of hundred miles daily. They're *here,* chirping and trilling and singing.

We made a bird feeder this year since the snow is lingering. It's big enough to serve all the new arrivals. We found a fifty-pound bag of Alaska barley that I've been storing for probably ten years ("Hey, what's this old bag in the corner under the pile of junk?"). It didn't look bad at all, but we had fresher supplies, so I brought it out for the birds. I dumped the bag in the front of the house, atop the snow.

Within hours ravens ripped the bag apart probably hoping it was the carcass of something. That left grain scattered widely.

Grey jays took over from there. They tossed grain around like Midas flinging gold. But the jays, like ravens, are year-round residents who know the lay of the land. The jays ignored the barley to clean the dog food bucket after I fed the dogs, their normal hand-out meal.

That left the migratory birds alone with all the seed. And they didn't flock to it. They continued to sit in the trees announcing their pleasure. They're *everywhere,* except in the front of the house.

They don't need my largesse. I don't know how they all manage in a spring like this one. But here they are.

This morning was another hard snow crust after a freezing night. And the birds didn't stop singing.

ʌʌʌ

Not long after the migratory birds arrived to make their nests the sky became filled with the sound of freedom.

That's what the young pilots who fly F-15s call a sonic boom. Elmendorf Air Force Base in Anchorage has a crew of young fighter pilots who fly F-15s. They've been taught, apparently, that bad guys hate loud noises. So to prevent enemy forces from swooping down to strafe Winnebagos traveling to Denali Park, the boys of the Alaska Strategic Air Command spent a lot of time this spring, for the first time since we've been here, blowing holes in the empty air over the remote parts of this valley by breaking the speed of sound.

They break it in two, in three, in Mach 4.

Trees shake. The ground trembles. Birds cower. Eggs rattle around in nests.

Our dogs all leap off their houses, atop which they've been lounging, to huddle inside. Our kids have shouted, without kidding, "Earthquake!" at particularly close booms. The new litter of pups tumble over each other like the Six Stooges trying to be first to get under the porch.

The young fighter pilots aren't content to rocket up above commercial jet paths to blow their sonic farts. They've flown way the hell out over the wilderness, after all, to practice maneuvers. They swoop low, they veer around chevrons of geese, and then, look! MIGs at four o'clock! C'mon Maverick, cover my tail. I'm goin' in! Faster! More speed! *Kabawhoooooom!*

Newborn moose calves whimper. Mother bears swat helplessly at trees.

I'm sure that these jet fighter aces have seen the Hollywood jet fighter movies repeatedly. But what they may have overlooked is the relatively barren desert sandstone background used for the jet fighter scenes. Down below those streaking celluloid F–15s is dusty rock, with horny toads. Down below the Alaska squadron's barrel rolls is more wildlife in a more fertile valley than almost anywhere else on earth. Lots of little forest babies all getting used to the serenity and beauty of the world. *Kabawhoooooom!*

Now, I'm certainly not suggesting that America's military readiness be compromised to save the baby animals from nightmares. This is a free country, and if they don't like what it takes to keep it that way they can migrate back to where they came from. But I'd like to remind our boys in the wild blue yonder that this part of Alaska is not a *barren* wilderness. I can imagine that when they get up in a plane roaring along at 900 m.p.h. the ground looks like a blur. But there are nesting bald eagles and denning wolverines and spawning salmon—plus a stray homesteader or trapper—who are first startled and then annoyed by the explosions.

So stick to the flight plans that head over ocean or unbroken ice fields, guys.

But then, I may just be crotchety about sudden noises from the sky. One midnight late in September with the sky dark with clouds I heard a low rumbling outside. It steadily increased in volume until the house was vibrating—dishes clattering on the shelves, tea splashing up from my cup. It was as if a twin-prop Chinook helicopter, the kind used for rescues on Denali, was hovering right overhead. But there was no whop-whop and whine of rotors, only a deep bass roar.

And lights! Blinking colored lights! I saw them through the window not far above the treetops moving slowly toward the mountains.

Then the lights began to circle and started coming straight back for the house.

I blew out my kerosene lantern. I jumped into my boots, threw on a down vest, grabbed the shotgun from above the door, and ran outside.

The UFO was huge. The ground shook. I stood behind a tree with my boots on the wrong feet clutching the shotgun.

When I realized that what passed a hundred feet directly overhead was a massive National Guard four-propeller C-130 cargo transport training plane I felt like a rube, a hillbilly, a bamboozled fool.

I hitched up my pants, spit my snuff on the ground, and shook my fist at the sky.

ᴧᴧᴧ

The intermediate season between spring and summer is called, in the north country, "breakup." The ice on creeks and lakes, the snow cover and fragile psyches all crumble.

Hard-packed trails dissolve to the consistency of over-cooked tapioca. Snow fields become mud. Bush planes are grounded, unable to land on their winter skis or summer floats until the ice finishes melting. Remote areas become cut off. A stroll to the outhouse becomes a slog up to the knees in cold slush.

Breakup, many people would agree, causes constipation.

I, however, have come to see it as one of the pleasures of living near the foothills of the Alaska Range. So what if travel is laborious by dogsled, impossible by snowmachine, even problematic by snowshoe because the snow is so wet and sticky the 'shoes sink with each heavy step to pick up ten pounds of viscous slop?

I like breakup for two reasons. The first took me years to appreciate. It's the reason that good can be found in even the worst of life's miseries. A thirteenth-century Japanese poet said it best: " 'Cause you ain't got no choice, Jack." I paraphrase.

The second reason is much easier to accept. Because it's so hard to go somewhere, I don't try to go anywhere. When I do

I end up sweaty and exhausted. So I don't. I have an excuse for doing nothing. So I do.

If it rains in the summertime I feel obligated to march around the homestead covering the things that should stay dry: firewood, tools, sleds. But during breakup everything is sunk ten inches deep in cold water anyway, so I just listen to the rain on the roof.

Many years ago I was feeling blue about a girlfriend who'd traded me in for a newer model. I was moping in an airport, waiting for a flight to Oblivion. Some guy with a guitar and a backpack offered me advice. The worst thing to do to a friend is offer advice. But offering it to a perfect stranger is okay.

"What you need, man," he said, "is like a little cabin in the woods where you wouldn't have to do anything except listen to the rain on the roof. No hassles. No grief."

Since our roof has a tendency to leak, there is some inevitable hassle. And since on a rainy day the kids prefer to play kickball and whiffle hockey inside the house, there's grief sooner or later, too. But otherwise that advice has held up pretty well, thanks to breakup.

Breakup's also the time when I make lists. Build new woodshed, clean storage cabin, write screenplay for successful kung-fu movie, win lottery—things like that. I don't even try to do any of them. If I did, I'd be doing something.

"Making lists" is a better answer to the question, "What are you doing?" than just admitting, "Nothing."

Ultimately, I'm relieved to accept the fact that there are some things over which I simply have no control. I can't fight the end of spring's beauty or the seasonal passage through breakup. It's good practice for taxes and aging and flat tires and unrequited love. It's a healthy exercise for those of us who brood about the ozone layer or follow the Cubs or would be kings.

Who cares if it's miserable to go anywhere when deep cold tapioca surrounds the house? Where else is there to go, when all is said and done, than home?

As more and more ground becomes green amidst the dwindling snow and less and less ice floats on the lakes I appreciate breakup increasingly. That's because the hordes of mosquitoes arise as soon as breakup's over.

The battle for my blood is one fight I've yet to accept as beyond my control.

ʌʌʌ **SUMMER**

Yesterday I killed two or three in the house. They drifted dreamily into my open hand—ha!—as if too new to life to know fear or desire.

Today my shirt-front is streaked with the black gruel of their corpses where I've wiped my hands after killing, and I've only been awake a few hours. They're at the windows, on the walls, rising up through cracks in the floorboards as if Judgment Day has come not with a trumpet blast but with a thin constant whine.

A hundred and seventeen mosquitoes I've killed since awakening—in the house alone! The truly macabre cannot be exaggerated.

The dogs lie mute outside with their paws over their noses. A gray sheen covers their backs, a thousand wings pressing against warmth. The mountains from this ridgetop look sharp against the sky, but it's illusion. When a sunshaft breaks through the drifting cumulus a mist of flying insects swirl within its column. My wife is patching the suspended, fine-mesh bed nets we sleep beneath in summer, as if our home were in Africa, or Amazonia.

This year's a bad one for bugs.

We read occasionally about an unexplained explosion of the snowshoe hare population in some part of Alaska, or an infestation of field mice. It makes interesting breakfast table conversation, speculating about cycles of fecundity.

But who can eat breakfast wearing a mosquito head-net?

Conversation is broken by repeated sudden *claps!* (118. Wipe.)

"In *Culex pungens*, the most common mosquito, the life-cycle is only ten days, so many generations are produced in a favorable season. But do not mistake life-cycle for life-history; mosquitoes may live as adults for several months." Slap that encyclopedia shut! (119, 120.)

A few days ago, before hiking home, I met a friend who lives farther to the south, in a boggy area. His blood–DEET level must have been 2.0, because he was raving about the bugs. "Never seen nothing like it! Clouds of bugs! Storms! I'm going to rent me a room in the Mush Inn until fall!" Ignorantly, I assumed our ridgeline would be above the buzz and bite.

Now I remember swatting at mosquitoes at 14,500 feet on Denali. I remember an old-timer talking about the summer he had to smear bug dope on his dogs' noses and they walked right into a grizzly, obliviously. I remember a bush pilot's summation of life out here when I told him I was going to build a home in the woods. "This land would be paradise if it weren't for the mosquitoes."

And my poor youngest son! It's a warm, bright day and I've swaddled him in enough clothing to sleep in snow. What kind of role model is a dad who hops around the house slapping himself in the head and shouting, "Ha!"

In urban Anchorage it's a lazy summer's day—a gentle breeze off the Inlet, the dreamy sound of a small plane far overhead. But here the forest thrums with the single oscillating note of a billion violinists gone mad. That endlessly repeated pitch is a desperate cry: "Suck blood or die! Suck blood or die!"

When I go outside I'll stand enclosed by encroaching vegetation, bound in layers of clothes, sweating rivulets of chemical repellent, listening to the insistent sound of a telephone that's been left off its hook too long while what little breeze that's passed through the overhanging trees dies against the small furred bodies enveloping my headnet.

Paradise? Bosch.

Still, there is this one positive discovery. I've finally solved the Zen riddle that monks have meditated upon for centuries: "What is the sound of one hand clapping?"

The answer: the last mosquito in the house being squeezed. Enlightenment!

∧∧

More than bugs in summer can seem overwhelming. The ceaseless daylight, the presence of grizzly bears, the imposingly rapid growth of plant life all require adaptive behavior (take two Valium and punt).

At first the speed with which the world becomes green is exciting. Each day is visibly different: fuller leaf, taller plants.

But within a few weeks of sprouting, the pace of growth becomes befuddling. It's similar to the anxiety about earthquakes: the world is shifting! Nothing is stable.

I've set a hoe down in the grass beside the garden and had it disappear within a few days, seemingly eaten by the grasses that top out at seven feet tall. Even if I cut the grass it continues to grow over my head unless I keep cutting, and keep cutting.

A lawn mower in this forest doesn't work. Even the expensive dwarf tractors that suburbanites drive are useless here. In addition to grass with stalks thick enough to support a seven-foot blade there are thorned devil's club with spiky foot-wide leaves, alder roots, rocks left by glaciers, bramble and brush.

I use a machete. Mine's made in Colombia, South America. When I use it I think of my *compañeros* in the jungle whacking at vines and lianas.

I could use a scythe, which has a long handle that saves one's lower back from the stooped swinging a machete requires. A scythe has the advantage of making its user feel like the Grim Reaper. That has a useful kind of energy in the annihilation of a half acre of thick foliage. But I tried a scythe once—a varnished oak $45 scythe—and after a dozen swings the thin blade was so dented by roots and rocks that I got $45 worth of satisfaction turning the handle into firewood.

Cutting the front yard can be unnerving as well as exhaust-ing. Pups romp in the grass where I'm whacking. Even if I cor-ral them in a pen I end up coincidentally slaughtering "good" plants—flowering fireweed, wild roses, varying berry plants. ("You killed the biggest watermelon berry plant!" wails one of our boys.) My swings, therefore, are tentative, which means that the insidious grasses don't get sliced flat but rather wrapped around the blade.

When I get frustrated and begin hacking wildly—eyes wide, gasping for breath—I end up feeling like an axe murderer.

To stop cutting altogether, however, would mean that soon we wouldn't be able to find *any* berry plants in the tangle, nor the house, nor our sanity.

So I've learned to wait until the time when we begin losing baseballs in the infield grass as well as the outfield, and then stand atop a birch tree stump to survey the yard, machete in hand. The yard rolls on to the Alaska Range on the distant horizon. When I then make my first pass of the summer through the grass of the small house clearing it doesn't feel like so big a task.

And if I do it right, by the final cut of the summer I'll have lots of berries to eat as I swing.

ʌ.ʌʌ

Maniacs in asylums grow gardens. So do nuns in cloisters and retired telephone operators in city apartments using seed advertised in the back of tabloid weeklies. Why, then, am I so amazed that our garden is finally, fully finished?

Because for the first time since moving into the forest it's conceivable to stop killing to survive: a hundred and twenty spruce for the house, salmon from the creek, alders from the view, a moose.

Because the mail-order Soil Testing Lab pronounced our soil "very poor" in four of four categories. Two feet below the "topsoil" is glacial till—chunks of the Alaska Range, barren rock of ages. At the time Leif Eriksson first set eyes upon the great green breast of the American continent our garden plot was moonscape swept by winds off the retreating glaciers. And now this most virgin land supports, tenuously, lettuce and cabbage and cauliflower and peas and carrots and broccoli and beets, dill and basil, comfrey.

Because a friend with two green thumbs who first discovered these acres decided, after long deliberation, not to live here. "Practically worthless," he pointed out, rolling glacial grit between his fingers.

Because years of chopping a frozen pile of rotting plants each summer so they'd thaw and make compost has resulted in a dark earth. There are even worms in it.

Because our youngest boy has abandoned the machete as his favorite outside toy in favor of digging down with his hands to pull up small wild plants, roots and all. "Let's put this in the garden, too!"

Because the rotary tiller I once rented never made it back here, stumped by fallen trees along the trail. With a mattock, then an axe and shovel, every bit of sod was turned, broken apart, and made ready. The job took years. It would have been a few days with a machine.

Because I grew up in the Midwest and have seen the stupefying amounts of poisons dumped on the withered plains to make the earth fertile again: ammonias and herbicides and the standard fertilizers that kill the rats dumb enough to eat the bags in silos. One in three Americans will get some form of cancer. I'm a biological time bomb primed with the chemicals I ate in my food as a child. But the kids will have half a chance now. Even broccoli is fun to eat, raw, picked right in the garden, as alluring as the blueberries on the ridge or the cloudberries on the tundra.

Because in addition to the predation of vegetable-loving hares and voles, moose need to be kept from eating the garden.

So far we've been successful using a brand of commercial deodorant soap hung around the plot. We heard that it effectively kept deer away. At least, that's what someone said that someone said they heard somewhere.

It all seems as amazing to me as eating dried papaya spears seemed on an Arctic Ocean dogsled expedition.

Hunting and fishing—killing for survival—is still very much a part of life in this world. But it always has been. Zucchini, now, that's something new.

ΛΛΛ

Once or twice every evening the dogs leap up to bark furiously. We look to where they're facing and see just alder leaves turning in the breeze, silvered curtains of birch, the green wall of the forest.

Miles away the snow mountains are plain above branch and leaf and bush. Fifty feet away could be a brown bear the size of a woolly mammoth and we'd never see it through the brush.

In the middle of the summer all the animals are ranging, newborns up and following parents to the best food sources, fattening up for the coming winter. Every creature is on the hunt.

An ermine in his summer coat of brown is living in the woodpile, reducing our mouse population.

Yesterday while Mom worked in the garden, the boys and I went out on the tundra. We took our three biggest male dogs as bear protection. Without a sound they began to slink toward a tree band, single file, ears flat, tails low, stalking. I called to them. They disappeared into the woods. I yelled again, louder.

The answer was a sudden horrible bleating, like a goat with its jugular cut for slaughter or a pig dangling from a noose. I told the kids to stay as I started running after the dogs. "What the hell?" was my dominant thought.

The cry came again and this time I knew what it was. The dogs had taken down a moose calf. I imagined the kids defying orders to follow me just as the calf's mother exploded out of the trees, trampling the boys. I screamed to all who might be listening, "Stop!"

Though I was at full adrenaline attention I still stumbled though the vegetation into the hollow where the calf lay, one dog at its throat, one on its haunch, the third growling at the cow to keep her at bay.

The cow bolted away. I began beating with my fists on the dogs, repeating, "Stop! No! No!" They cowered. I was the Alpha wolf of the pack, though if they'd wanted they could have turned on me in a dominance fight to the death. They didn't. The calf wobbled away. The dogs wagged their tails.

Most everyone out here carries a gun. I've seen a ten-year-old with a .45; his dad was "learnin' him young." There are one or two naturalists who carry only faith or a quote from John Muir's wilderness travel diaries: "Be gone!" But only the grizzlies aren't apprehensive about moving through this land, and they run the risk of being shot on sight for "self-protection."

Sometimes when we leave home with all the dogs we return to bear sign: paw prints on a window, a shredded outhouse seat. Occasionally we take the 12-gauge shotgun and push our way through the brush toward whatever the dogs are barking at, just to see what we can see. We've not surprised anything yet in our thrash and crash.

Last week we hiked to the road to find, halfway out, on the shore of the big tundra lake, the beaver lodge ripped open, mud and sticks strewn around the gaping hole in the mound as if a bomb had hit it. The scaly skin of a beaver tail lay atop the ruins. A hundred yards away we found part of its skull, one long curved yellow tooth sticking up from the ground. "Was he a *friendly* bear?" asked my five-year-old, glancing around. So much for the Pooh books.

Eat or be eaten, range widely but be discreet. These are truths of the forest that are obvious. A rational fear, too, is unavoidably a part of this world—not panic but focus, heightened awareness. Anything could be out there, and probably is.

ΛΛΛ

The tundra, too, hides unexpected life. As I sat like Gulliver atop the six-inch-tall dwarf birch in bright sun, a dragonfly landed on my wrist. With eyes covering three-quarters of its head it stared at me, at the sky, at the lake beside which I sat— all at the same time, unblinking. The daylight made me squint. The dragonfly had no eyelids. When I'd slowly raised my hand to a few inches from my nose I could see the sun reflected in its eyes—a hexagonal sun outlined in cobalt blue with prismatic dots swirling within.

"Reflected in its eyes" suggests a mirroring, but what I saw was an iridescent flowing design, an impressionist's interpretation of reality. If that's how a dragonfly sees the sun, then my face too was hexagonal, swirled with color. How many of the great modern painters now dead have begged to be reborn as a dragonfly?

And how in the world can so much light be absorbed unfiltered, uninterrupted? That's my new definition of glory: no convoluted temporal lobe encased in bone to analyze a beautiful day, just eyes as big as ski goggles open to the oscillating sun.

The grasses this year have grown taller than I've seen before. I tugged up a handful of stems from the edge of the tundra and found a deeper root system, reaching into the wetlands. Even the seeds of the grasses are fuller, billows of flaxen grain. That bounty can't be harvested, milled, and baked. The large herbivores that live here don't eat the grasses either. Moose, caribou, beavers, even omnivorous bears ignore the grasses. Woolly mammoths might have gorged on this plant, but now it serves no major economic or aesthetic role. So I try to see the grass as perfect just as it is, benefitting only itself, an earthly presence of no special value but abundantly alive, as any of us would wish to be.

Even the swamp spruce, the stunted straggled trees in stray

places across the tundra, are showing growth. They can live a hundred years and reach no taller than a boy: boreal bonsai.

We've learned that picking up any thin branch or trunk from where it's settled into the tundra, half-buried in moss, requires a quick shake to knock off the small red ants that eat from it. At the end of this summer I turned over a swamp spruce "raft" the boys had cobbled together (to use more as a submarine than boat in the swimming lake) and had to drop it. Ants were streaming up my arms. The implication is that ants live *everywhere* on the tundra.

What I find so remarkable is that the tundra is wet. Anywhere we sit is damp. It becomes a huge shallow pool after a heavy rain. That's what its plant life has adapted to: constant moisture.

The fact that the ants live underwater, as it seems, veined throughout the matted root systems, is as impressive as their numbers. There are few ants that live in the dark soil of the forest, where ants "should" live.

In the reference works I've checked I've found no description of red Alaska tundra ants. This is not a surprise given the fact that there are some 8,000 species of ants worldwide. I'm reminded that what we do know of the natural world is outweighed by what we don't.

The only natural predator of these ants that I've noticed is a plant, the sundew (*Drosera anglica*). Sundew grow pervasively on the tundra. The plant is just a few short stalks ending in small oval leaf pads ringed by sticky red drops like dew. When an ant gets stuck, the plant digests it, mandibles and all, open to the sun, under the unblinking gaze of dragonflies.

Soon a cold front will come through, low gunmetal stratus clouds covering the sun, often for weeks, with a steady chilly drizzle falling. Like a theater being emptied, the bugs and birds and flora will wane until, in what always feels sudden, countless eyes have closed.

⋀⋀⋀ FALL

It floods in the fall every few years. In rain forests it rains. The last big flood washed out the bridge on the gravel mining road at Moose Creek. "Washed out," though, sounds like a stain lifted from dirty clothes. The steel girders twisted and burst, the bracketing railroad ties snapped like saplings in the path of a bulldozer, re-bar was smashed from concrete.

A little trout stream did that.

The ridge where we live was created by flood. When the glaciers receded, their meltwater poured rivers across bare rock, digging hollow, leaving hill. Even now, after a heavy rain, creeks gouge new channels, collapse banks.

Flood is common, but it's still eerie.

The maritime climate of this valley lofts successive cloud systems from the ocean all summer. During the summer countless billions of gallons of rainfall get sucked up into the vegetation. In the fall, however, when the green forest floor has collapsed to brown mulch, a stray "summer" frontal system dumps its rains atop ground that hurries it unimpeded into the creeks. A couple of those dumps back to back sends the creeks over their banks.

The roar of dark water down the ridge from the house is at first startling. It's loud. Without much foliage to filter the sound it's like a great waterfall. Then, as occasional heavy splashes of falling trees and pieces of bank punctuate the background rumble, it becomes morbid. That's our world crumbling away down there!

Floods, big or bigger, are inevitable here. First come the cold monsoons. The roof will leak from the constant rain, the house become musty. Fungus will bloom on the woodpile. The root cellar will be filled with a foot of stagnant water. The blue mood of sodden afternoons will last into the night as gusts of rain beat on the greenhouse fiberglass and wake us from dreams.

The listlessness induced by long cold rains at times can seem as disturbing as flood. When we go outside in rain gear to do the necessary dog feeding or wood splitting, we go slow, plodding perfunctorily. Then we sit around listening for the creek to rise into roar, muttering, "This could be it."

But finally, when it does flood, emotional priorities are set straight. "My God! We're trapped! The creek can't be crossed!"

How long will it last? How much land will be lost? Will the bridge go, too?

Salmon eggs laid in the gravel of the stream beds will be washed out to sea. Four or five years hence, when those eggs' fish would have returned to bear *their* young, the surface of the creek won't be rippled with the wakes of many sleek silver torpedoes.

It's been raining for five days straight now. The forecast is vague: intermittent showers, cloudy, partly cloudy. But I can smell big rains coming. The creek is up.

This could be it.

/\/\/\

The most incredible result of this year's Hundred Year Flood is that so little was affected.

I flew over the hardest-hit parts of the valley while the flood was still carving chunks out of railroad and highway bridges. I saw holes where the foundations of houses had been, log jams festooned with propane tanks and refrigerators and twisted sheets of roofing metal, a floating dog house trailing a chain with a bloated dog still attached, a field once russet turned the silvered blue of a reflecting pool.

Each of the hundreds of creeks in the upper valley swelled six to ten feet high and fifty to one hundred feet across, then maintained that phenomenal volume for twenty-four hours. National Guard helicopters rescued families in remote areas. The town of Talkeetna became a small refugee camp.

And yet when the waters receded it wasn't the destruction that was most startling. It was what remained.

I walked my creek two days after the flood's high point. The fact that ground remained underfoot at all was mildly astonishing. Grass was pressed as flat as fur on a seal's back where it hadn't been torn out by the roots and strung from tree limbs at head height. The trunk of a massive cottonwood was wedged between two bowed spruce, held off the ground like a see-saw.

But the more I walked the creek bank the more bank I saw remained. Certainly sections were sloughed away, but I began to notice not the few mud pits where trees had been blown out of the earth but the many trees that still overhung the water, the berry bushes that still lined the shore, moss that was greener than a week before.

After a few miles I stopped looking altogether for signs of devastation. I climbed the ridge flanking the creek for an overview.

The landscape looked groomed: birch leaves all raked against bushes, years-worth of windblown branches swept from the meadows. In floods as in earthquakes, it's mainly man's constructions that are "devastated." The natural world had been changed only where it was natural: at the bend of a creek, where sagging trees once stood in poor soil. Even the temporary shallow lakes would drain, leaving little altered.

When I came to the point where our "bridge" crossed the creek I got my biggest surprise. The old giant cottonwood hadn't budged. It still lay across the stream. A piece of bark was torn off. The creek's channels had been rearranged beneath it, new sloughs cut around it. Flood detritus was stacked against its roots and its remaining large branches. There was no question that brown water had plowed over it, digging at roots that remained woven into the bank. A climbing rope I'd strung as a makeshift handrail three feet above the trunk was draped with bits of the forest floor. If anything was in the dead center of the flood, it was this fallen tree.

I walked across it, then back, then across it again, marvelling. The past week has reminded us again of the power of flood. But enormously greater is the continuity of the world.

ΛΛΛ

September is the month to get the homestead ready for winter.

It's approaching the middle of October now, and I'm still getting ready.

In part that's because there can never be too much wood split and dried. One of the historic Far North indicators of an old timer's cabin is a *huge* supply of cordwood stacked neatly around the house. I'm not seasoned enough, I guess, to be compulsive about wood splitting, but I do work at it along with the other pre-winter chores.

The dogsleds need to be rebuilt where they've been beaten up: cracked wood stanchions, broken lashings, the curved brush bow in the front of the sled split from hitting one too many trees head on. The roofs of the various buildings need to be patched with tar or metal or sod so the snow load freezing to the roof doesn't, when it begins to melt from radiant house heat, come dripping into the house. New stove cement will keep the firebrick together when logs get shoved into the firebox in rapid succession on particularly cold days. House logs can use fresh chinking where winds could blow through.

If all this work seems like preparation for war, for a long siege, it is. Once the first big snow comes there's no retreat. I've been caught off-guard before. Every third day all winter long up on the roof with a hammer and ice axe chopping loose constantly accumulated ice dams from the dormers is a losing battle. When the water starts dripping onto the bed in the middle of the night during a wind storm, I've lost.

There is one aspect of getting ready for winter that gets easier day after day. As brittle grasses and ferns and fallen leaves gradually settle to the land's contours rather than obscuring them, much that was lost becomes found.

I just discovered, for instance, a quarter-cord of birch—fifteen thick sections of trunk dumped from the freight sled after the last wood haul of spring. I dumped the load a little way from the house when the sled sagged off the trail. It was easier to roll 700 pounds of wood into the wet snow rather than wrestle the sled back onto packed footing. Besides, I knew where the wood was. Duh. Who could misplace something so big?

Oops. I knew there was more wood around somewhere to split. But it was simpler to wait for the vegetation to collapse to locate it.

Also exposed has been a machete, a hammer, a metal washtub, a wheelbarrow, a badminton racquet, two dinner plates, and a hundred sodden paper airplanes.

"Are you guys picking up all those airplanes you've been shooting off the back porch?"

"Uh-huh."

Each day of late fall is a treasure hunt. In ever widening circles stuff turns up, sometimes from years before. It's like a long Easter: celebrating what's been resurrected.

Wandering the ridge in discovery, chopping wood, sitting up on the roof with patching tools—all of it requires being outside. That's what keeps the chores from becoming a pain. The ochre landscape extending to recently revealed horizons is serene after so much looming greenery. The north wind is alive: the breath of glaciers. The moon has returned.

ᴧᴧᴧ WINTER

On nights like this, with the temperature twenty below and the north wind blowing in black gusts, rattling the windows, I fall into survival mode.

Survival is anticipation, the practice of looking ahead to troubleshoot before trouble arises, rehearsing possible scenarios so the course of action is known no matter what might happen. Of course, the unexpected is usually what happens, but survival can be less complicated if most potential complications are anticipated.

For instance, what if the next gust of wind blew a busted branch through a window? The wind chill outside is seventy or eighty below zero. It'd be like breaking a porthole on a jetliner at 20,000 feet. The kids upstairs, being read to sleep by their mother, would be powdered in spindrift, their faces quickly reddened, their alarm extreme.

First I'd grab a parka and gloves (I'm wearing my boots; the floor is cold), stick a handful of nails in a pocket, and then go wrestle a piece of plywood to the window hole. If the big picture window broke, no piece of scrap plywood is large enough to cover it. Snowblocks would work, since the snow that's already slid from the roof is densely packed and as high as the bottom of the window. With the wind deflected I could staple up plastic sheeting.

Worse-case scenario in this weather, though, would be if the stove gave out. Not *went* out. Died. The bottom's been rusting from creosote drip for a couple of winters already, and if it fell off, then what? Then...I'd try to patch it with some aluminum flashing left over from the roof dormers, easy to cut with shears. Even better would be to cannibalize the sheet metal off the little air-tight stove in the greenhouse, keep warm using the hack-saw.

Eskimos traditionally heated their small sod homes on the arctic coast with a single flame from a seal-oil-fueled lamp of stone. No way this wood and glass house could be habitable without a heavy-duty cast-iron stove.

That's the discouraging part of my survival-mode game: it's hard to imagine living deep in the forest for long without the technology of the wider world. I use stove metal and eightpenny nails and fiberglass insulation and petroleum oil and HiShok 12-gauge magnum lead slugs.

But what would happen if suddenly we got cut off from the supplies that seem so necessary? What if, God forbid, America should go the way of the Mayans and Egyptians and Mongols and Romans and Incas and Persians and Vikings and Ozymandias and—

And so survival mode takes a quantum leap. Instead of figuring ways to patch up my existing technology, I find myself considering deadfalls and snares and bone fishhooks. There are lots of beaver out there for fur. Even in a severe winter moose are plentiful.

Survival depends upon the largesse of the economic world. That doesn't mean just supermarkets and hardware stores and the Tokyo stock exchange. That means the economics of caribou migrations and salmon runs and moose populations and the availability of firewood and the climate patterns of the shifting seasons.

So often I take for granted the ease of life when life is easy. It seems to be only when things get rough that I admit how precarious all our lives are, how dependent on forces far beyond our control so much is, daily.

The best I can do at those particularly precarious times— wind rattling, branches snapping, snow whipping—is to sit still, breathe slowly, and listen. I might not hear any answers, but recognizing the steadiness of my own breath is a start.

∧∧∧

Every winter the same refrain starts in more than a few residents of this landscape: "It's so *dark!* The winter is so long and dark!"

When I first lived through a boreal winter I was so surprised by the ambient light of December and January and February that I was baffled by those who complained about their Seasonal Affective Disorder—the emotional malady that results in some from lack of sunlight.

What I saw was moonlight in silverpoint brilliance, green auroral waves as mysterious as imagination, blued starlight so radiant off the snow cover that I found it unnecessary to use a headlamp on night dogsled runs in or out of the homestead. Who could miss the plain old yellow sun?

I figured that the whiners were people who never viewed their world without electric lamps or car headlights or flashlights or the flickered glow of satellite-dish television in the bars.

Finally I've admitted that there really are people who are seriously distressed by the winnowing of daylight. They get moody and withdrawn because the winter sun teases on the southern horizon, ducking low.

My genes are Mediterranean, where the December sun is warm and the hills blaze bronze. And I look forward to winter more than to summer.

At this latitude, as the winter sun slips lower in the field of the sky, the moon takes its place, staying up longer, higher, brighter. With almost any kind of moon up, the mountains from the mid-valley Susitna River are as clear as the flying buttresses of Notre Dame from the Seine.

Sunlight? Thank goodness it's taking a seasonal break. Diffused stained glass has its beauty, too.

That's why I still think many of the constant complaints about the "darkness" are a crock. What's lacking is not light, but joy. An honest appreciation of the subtleties of winter (and forty below temperatures or thirty m.p.h. north winds are not subtle) creates so much up mood that brooding is difficult.

The images of the boreal winter—moon above tapering spruce, white glaciers, blue mountains—are powerful archetypes. It's hard to stand under a full moon in a silent spruce forest and feel glum. It takes an effort to ignore the wonder of skiing up high tundra toward glaciers.

When I have to spend much time in a city I grouse, "Too many headlights and streetlights." That stance is a crock, too. There are certainly ways to look at any environment and see its beauties.

I'm just particularly sensitive to the facile view that winter is dark. It's like entering Notre Dame or Chartres, gazing up at the medieval stained glass, and whispering, "Why is it so dark in here? They should turn on some lights."

The real dark of winter is not in the sky but in our heads. Once we decide to look, the light can't be avoided, anywhere.

ΛΛΛ

My little sister, who lives on the big island of Hawaii, has just sent a glossy color catalog of her boyfriend's paintings. He's into tropical landscapes, as is to be expected: green volcanoes and white sand beaches, sunsets and sarongs, all in Day-Glo colors.

I've been looking at the catalog by the afternoon light of an overcast December day. This light, by comparison, pales next to the vibrancy of the equatorial sun. At times the light here seems exhausted by the time it fights its way from the distant horizon through bare tree branches and cold. It lies against my hand shivering. Because of the tilt of the earth, it has angled through the atmosphere thousands of miles farther to reach here than it needs to simply plop down like ripe fruit on Hawaii.

But as I've looked up from bright acrylic hibiscus to flat snow it's apparent that this winter light is *everywhere.* It's not broken by deep shadows. It's not blocked by overhanging vegetation. Instead of a spotlight, it's a pervasive luminescence. Instead of a 1,000 watt bulb hanging from the center of the sky, it's a glow that's spread across the heavens like the Magellanic Cloud on clear, cold nights.

Walk around a spruce and there'll be the same soft radiance on all sides. Walk around a coconut palm and there'll be sun and shade, hot and cool, bright and dim.

Some say that the world is made up of opposing forces, the forces of light and the forces of darkness. Those who first said that, however, came from the desert, where the day is glaring and the night is pitch. The Eskimos, on the other hand, say that the world is all of a piece—land and sea fused at the edges in ice, animal blood becoming human blood, heaven and earth interwoven. Their world, most of the year, is subtly lit.

This light is not explosive with flashy scarlets and coruscating metallic golds. High skies and smooth snow is dreamy, serene: subtle shades of blue. I can understand why Gaugin, who made his life and reputation painting gaudy Tahitian landscapes, left on his easel, when he died, a snowscape.

I don't know if there's a paint made that can capture the elusiveness of this northern winter color. Maybe that's why so much Alaska art is schlock. Dogsleds and polar bears and grinning Eskimos on black velvet is the standard stuff of tourist galleries.

Once I met a couple from New York's SoHo who had come to Alaska to record on video "the best" of Alaska's art. I thought, "Finally. The serious art world has discovered the possibilities of this lambent light." I launched into a rap about how magical the light is in winter where I live, its intricacies and complexities. They tugged on their matching safety-pin earrings, shuffled their black high-top Keds, and looked distracted. "We *like* grinning Eskimos and polar bears," they said. "It's, you know, totally camp. Perfect kitsch."

When I was a kid my favorite thing to draw, not counting the tanks and airplanes that shot at each other on my blue-lined notebook paper during bored grade-school afternoons, were palm trees. I still doodle palm trees when I'm commanded by one of my sons to "draw something with me." For a child of the Midwest, like me, palm trees are fantasy images not unlike the moon above snow mountains, which is the only other drawing I can turn out on demand.

But in December here the light is so rarified I don't know how any art could capture it except in intimation.

It's like a traditional Chinese watercolor: part air, part cloud, part imagination.

Easy to see. Hard to touch.

⋀⋀⋀ Daily Life

After visiting an elegantly appointed urban duplex recently, I've been noticing that our own homestead interior decor is, as they say in pastel drawing rooms, *"très crappe."*

It's not that I leave my socks on the floor or anything. It's just that the furnishings haven't been planned. They sort of happened, like berry plants growing from seeds dropped in bear scat. Ideally, to save face, this "form follows function" method of design can be seen to echo the world outside, which grows rampant, leaving beauty to be perceived, not determined.

For instance, in place of a Ming-dynasty porcelain vase umbrella stand by the front door, I have arranged two five-gallon metal dog food buckets flecked with clods of dried animal fat. Behind them, waiting to be revealed when I go out to feed, hang from a six-penny nail three trashed chainsaw chains classically colored in rust and old oil.

This "real life" motif is echoed throughout the house. To the right of the chains is a bright red fire extinguisher, contrasted intriguingly by an adjacent yellow-and-blue can of WD-40.

Warhol painted Campbell's soup cans; Oldenburg sculpted huge baseball bats. Their ordinary art now fetches tremendous sums. One day I hope that my arrangements, too, will be discovered.

In a corner opposite the door, crawling the wall like a vine from the floor, are, in ascending order, ten dog harnesses, a broken wood snowshoe, a seat harness with six carabiners clipped in, a fifty-meter rainbow-colored climbing rope and, atop that growth, clutching at nails and log knots, a strand of popcorn left over from Christmas.

Some would see randomness in this design. But it's no more random than the forest outside where every bough and blade has been planned by causality. The cause in that corner was to get things out of the middle of the floor. The only female energy in the house, the boys' mother, is centrifugal in that regard.

Above that middle of the floor is a truly unique piece of functional decorating. To make an ad hoc jungle gym for the boys I strung sixty feet of tubular webbing and eighty feet of half-inch Manila hemp rope. The lines attach to the staircase on one side of the house, run up through the log joists supporting the upstairs floor, then across the room to tie into support poles for the roof.

It's a big spider's web. At first it was an effort to walk anywhere downstairs because the route required ducking low beneath or stepping high over line. But until it comes down in favor of some new game, we're almost used to it. I'm still unnerved, though, when a kid swings over my head like Tarzan. Kinetic art is making a comeback in the sedentary 1990s, I hear.

In any well-considered house the walls are hung with framed paintings. We've followed suit, though without the frames.

On one wall is a stunning diversity of art in varying media: finger paint, crayon, colored pencil, and pastel chalk. The colored pencil works are neo-Jackson Pollock: abstract scribbles of color. The crayon sketches are in a primitive style, like Grandma Moses' after she had her final stroke. The finger paintings actually contain one foot painting: five little toes squooshed amidst a field of mud brown.

On a flanking wall is a large four-foot-square color photo of the eye of God. It was taken from a NASA landsat satellite. Blue glaciers radiate like striations in an iris from the piercing and luminous center which the U.S. Geologic Survey describes, at the bottom of the photo, as "Mt. McKinley, Denali National Park and Preserve." We affixed a little gold stick-um star to a spot on the eyelashes (actually long dark creeks) where our house is.

Above the photo hangs a two-man, six-foot cross-cut saw because…because there was nothing else up there.

Modestly I can say that none of this decor took very long to conceive. It was done because a place was needed to put the stuff.

But my socks aren't on the floor.
They're hanging on a nail behind the stove.

/\/\/\

When I moved into the virgin forest I swore up and down that I'd *never* have a homestead like virtually every other I'd seen in Alaska, where junk accumulated in the yard, and remained: rusted machines (bulldozers to Roto-tillers), used fifty-five-gallon fuel drums, old tree stumps and knotted burls too thick to split, abandoned dogsleds and the broken kitchen sink.

Amidst the intricate order of the natural world I saw that stuff for what it was: garbage.

The Japanese have a word, *aware* (ah-wah-ray), that means, "the beauty of things that pass." It crops up a lot in their classical poetry. The word describes things such as an autumnal leaf falling, a weathered piece of wood, the lined face of an old woman.

The grace of that concept has helped me accept the fact that I've got junk strewn all over the place. (May the lightning bolt miss me to strike the old stove pipes instead.)

Now I see beauty in a rusted half of a fifty-five-gallon drum, once a planter in the greenhouse. The colors of oxidation are actually lovely, but what I mostly see is the memory of its place in our lives. When it no longer held soil the kids tried to use it as a backstop for their .22 rifle target practice. It sort of worked for a while, at least making a cool sound when they hit it, then got rolled beside the woodshed.

In Chicago's central Civic Center plaza, remember, is the city's famous Picasso sculpture. Its tons of iron are the exact color of my rusted drums.

I've also come to *like* the way stumps and abandoned dogsleds litter the yard. Originally I had envisioned a manicured lawn with rows of flowers and trailing berries at the edges. We've got the trailing berries, but they're all over, even entwining the stumps and abandoned dogsleds. The idea of a manicured *anything* out here by now is bizarre.

In big cities the elegant chrome and glass skyscrapers are polished and buffed each night by crews of uniformed maintenance workers. But still on the streets around the buildings are all kinds of human detritus: plastic grocery bags, foam hamburger containers, squashed soda cans, homeless alcoholics. Ravens collect bright shiny objects; people abandon stuff that's lost its utility.

"If they don't want you to toss stuff in the street why do they send trucks around to sweep it up?" an urban acquaintance once asked.

It must be a human impulse, then, not just a homestead habit. Dump it where you stand. Let someone else (the Sanitation Department, Mother Nature) clean it up.

Have you ever seen someone purposefully walk a half block out of his way to reach a garbage can, toss a candy wrapper from a foot away, miss, and then turn to walk on? That's me. Good intentions mixed with human habit.

But at least in the boreal forest the things I leave lying around acquire a quality of *aware* that plastic grocery bags don't. A moss-streaked moose rack covered with trailing berries looks better than a flattened styrofoam filet-o-fish container.

That's a lame excuse for dumping junk in the yard.

But I've found myself idly picking through stuff carried over to the bonfire area by my wife or kids after a flurry of cleaning. In addition to flammable trash we burn used metal—cans or broken buckets or old typewriter ribbon spools—to hasten the oxidation back to earth. This pan with the snapped handle though? I could probably use that for a dogfood scooper. I'll just chuck it over there. And the brake assembly from the old sprint sled! I built that! I'd better take this cracked stanchion, too. It's red oak, kiln dried. I remember when I rolled the sled going down devil's club hill, whacked that stanchion full against a spruce and only cracked it. This part of a moose pelvis, now, one of the dogs can gnaw on that. And...

Let's face it. Remote Himalayan people covet trekkers' empty corned beef tins to pound flat for roofing. Masai warriors lift used thirty-five mm film canisters to insert into their decoratively stretched ear lobes (stuff can be *put* in that kind of body ornamentation), most anything can have a utilitarian value in the right place and time.

And beauty does exist in much that gets discarded.

Λ.Λ.Λ

As the Finns say about their greatest contribution to the world, the sauna, "Vavooom-jor."

At least I think that's what they say. The 1948 classic text, *The Finnish Sauna,* points out that "the only word to pass from Finnish into common usage is 'sauna.'"

Other languages have given us numerous common words. "Spaghetti" and "Sophia Loren" from the Italian. "Banzai" and "Walkman" from the Japanese. "Expos" and "Blue Jays" from the Canadian.

But the Finns, a taciturn bunch, have condensed everything worth communicating to a foreigner into one word: sauna.

Before homesteading, I thought that saunas, like racquetball courts and juice bars, were mostly found in certain athletic clubs. All the saunas I'd seen before moving to Alaska were the same: a warmish little room with slatted benches. Inside, a half dozen small rocks always lay atop an electric space heater, above which was a sign: "Do Not Throw Water On Rocks."

Everyone threw water on rocks. As often as not the sauna had another sign outside the door that said, "Out Of Order."

Then I came to the North Woods and discovered that saunas were as common as dog teams and snow storms. Since all of the saunas were wood-heated rather than electric they were in regular use.

Almost everyone I met who lived in the woods had a sauna or had a neighbor who had a sauna. Some saunas had slatted benches, some had plywood seats. Some were crafted finely, some looked like they were built by a seven-year-old with a hacksaw and Elmer's glue. Like mine. But they all got hot enough to say, "Vavooom!"

Traditional Scandinavian saunas were both for getting clean and for socializing. Same thing in my neck of the north. Maybe the popularity of saunas across the circumpolar regions is because showers tend to run cold at thirty below, and as long as the trouble's been taken to locate dead standing spruce, fell it, split it, stoke the sauna stove, heat enough water for a bath, and wait until the room is hot enough to get undressed, you might as well invite some friends to socialize.

"The traditional sauna does not segregate the sexes, and is kept hot enough to dispense with superficial clothing," says the guidebook. This allows for some pretty unconventional socializing. Athletic clubs don't follow this traditional sauna practice for fear of getting shut down by the cops. But at 200 degrees, with sweat stinging the eyes and all muscles hanging limp, it's impossible to socialize too much.

The second-best part of the sauna comes after getting so hot that it's hard to stand without oozing to the floor. In winter the practice here is to then roll naked in the snow. In summer a bucket of spring water poured over the head is almost as effective. The result is like bungee-jumping: heart-poundingly shocking but exhilarating. It's like being trampled by beautiful naked Amazons: initially and brutally numbing, but then, gazing up stupefied from the ground, oh what a lovely sight!

Admittedly, this is a rather extreme alternative to a simple shower. But then living in the circumpolar forest is a rather extreme alternative to a simple city.

A real sauna does, however, get one clean, like being tied to the hood of a car before sending it through an automatic wash. Scandinavians traditionally flayed themselves with birch branches to "stimulate circulation." I've not personally seen anyone adopt this custom, perhaps because some of us know when enough is enough.

But I've been in our sauna when the air temperature was 230 degrees. I was not in the 230-degree sauna for long. A little of that goes a long way, like microwave cooking.

Afterward, after the rolling in the snow and the wooziness and the exhilaration, I've felt reborn: pink and smooth and a little stunned.

At that point the traditional wisdom counsels a long rest. Manual labor is difficult if not impossible, thinking is reduced to the basics (inhale then exhale, open eyes to see and close eyes to sleep) and worries about the world seem to recede with consciousness. There's not much alternative but to take a long rest.

That's the best part.

/\/\/\

"You mean you don't have electricity?" people would ask.

I'd confess that no, in fact we didn't.

Their faces would get this funny look, as though trying to stifle a reaction that might embarrass me.

They wanted to say, "How primitive," or "That's terrible," but instead they'd say, "How...quaint."

I didn't mind being taken for eccentric or indigent. I *liked* not having electricity. I ran the stereo with flashlight batteries. The oil lamp cast a beautiful amber light. The root cellar was a fine refrigerator.

What I did mind was that almost no one grasped that we didn't *need* electricity.

When I lived in Manhattan, the world's most electric island, what I had in my apartment that required electricity was a stereo and lights and a refrigerator. That's all. I did not have a television, a microwave, a vacuum cleaner, a Cuisinart, a word processor, a garbage disposal, an air conditioner, or a telephone answering machine. I didn't want that stuff. I didn't need any of it.

I still don't need it. When New York City experienced its complete power outage one night in the summer of 1976 the scene was from a nightmare: people screaming, headlights careening, panic, terror. When there's a complete power outage here it comes from blowing the lantern out. Moonlight shines in.

What's so critical about having electricity anyway? We've got a great cookstove and a good broom and plenty of sharp knives for fancy kitchen work and voracious dogs that dispose of the garbage. The first appliance Third World villages buy when they become electrified is a television, but we in the know have long understood that television causes ozone layers and cancer of the rain forests. Or something like that. It's not healthy, though. That's what I keep telling my kids.

Electricity is the most overrated benefit of industrialization. Chernobyl was the result of the infatuation with electricity. Three Mile Island. Los Angeles

So then how can I explain our new, complete solar panel electrical system, a 900 lumen bulb of which I'm using to write?

Simple: hypocrisy. Actually, I got worried that those lovely kerosene lanterns were throwing toxic fumes into the house. And the closest seal from which to render oil is 500 miles north.

Solar panels are supposed to last just about forever, too. Petroleum and coal get used up, diesel generators wear out, but in the year 3000 the solar-powered red warning lights at Alaska Railroad crossings will still flash every time a mutant cockroach rumbles down the track.

Another self-justifying reason for the solar panel system is because it costs nothing after the initial investment. No fuel expenses, no maintenance.

Non-polluting free power forever. Doesn't it sound great?

But there's a catch. Having a complete electrical system assumes having an array of electrical appliances. We still run just lights and the stereo. And in the summer there's no need for artificial light.

For a while I brooded about having sold out, about being part of the problem that mandated flooding beautiful Glen Canyon and strangling the Columbia River and altering many other places just to build dams for electricity. For a few maniacal years recently there was a plan to dam the Susitna River for power, and a generation before that the same mentality seriously considered damming the Yukon (to light up Rudolph's nose?).

"Don't worry," counselled the folks who sold the solar-power system to us. "You're off the grid now."

We were never on the grid. In fact, there isn't even a grid anywhere near here.

But at least we're no longer using a steady supply of cadmium D-cells that end up being carried to distant landfills. Nor do we burn much fossil fuel. There's some small integrity in that.

Though my refusal to rig up a sixty-foot-tall antenna for television is still plain obstinance.

∧∧∧

On our stereo/cassette/radio boom box, now spouting wires from its empty battery compartment that run upstairs to the solar panel array, we can occasionally receive a radio signal from an Anchorage television station. Why we get the audio from a far-distant TV station I don't know. Perhaps it's because the surrounding mountains are veined with quartz, which transceive the signal, amplifying it. Radio Moscow during auroral displays comes in, too. But not much else, which is why the TV signal is so notable.

I also don't know which television station we receive, KDUM or KYUK or KDOG. The only thing I've watched on television in many years is a game or two of the World Series, at a local bar.

But I do know that the station has cartoons on Saturday mornings. When I first discovered the signal buried at the farthest left extreme of the dial I realized that the very loony tunes garbling from the speakers were just that. In the flush of old boyhood memories, I called one of our sons over and announced, "These are cartoons!"

He listened enthralled for about ten minutes and then said,

"This is dumb if you can't see 'em."

Anyone who might worry about the negative effect on kids of Saturday morning cartoon shows only has to cover the screen with a towel and just listen. Dialogue is a sporadic, imbecilic, non sequitur interpolated into *booooiiings* and *wheeees* and *blams*. The only coherent articulate messages are, of course, the commercials, which are emphatic. The Smurfs and Sylvester and Bugs and Porky Pig and their many peers all talk like babies, squeaking and slurring and spluttering. But when the bass-voiced announcer intones, "Buy one now!" it's like the voice of God.

That night we investigated a television drama. Most dramas are predicated upon speech. On television, however, our one limited example was based on bum-bum-*bum-bum*-BUM-*BUM*, followed by a dissonant orchestral chord overdubbed with a shriek or a gunshot. I accept that television is a visual medium, but shouts and grunts and explosions and buh-*BUMMM* must be more expository than language.

I certainly can't judge whether television is—if it can actually be seen—stimulating or vacuous. But I am sure that we all make our own worlds. Even those who don't believe they have a choice about their place or circumstance or situation have made it so.

It seems loony to let others portray the world in shorthand, to reduce great variation to a soundtrack formula. The result can only be confinement, a frustration that what's offered as reality isn't real.

λλλ

The spruce beetle, *Dendroctonus rufipennis,* like gonococcus, *Neisseria gonorrhoeae,* is a scourge of our own doing.

Some foresters will insist that spruce beetle infestations just *happen,* the result of fate, inevitably and naturally.

This is like insisting, "I must have gotten the clap from that old toilet seat."

A current U.S. Department of Agriculture booklet on spruce beetles states, "When beetle populations increase to high levels in downed trees, beetles may enter susceptible, large diameter, standing timber."

The beetle prefers to burrow into the bark of downed spruce because trees on the forest floor are shaded; direct sunlight can kill beetles within their host trees. When the supply of fallen trees is high enough to generate a good population of beetles, surrounding living trees catch their swarming flight, and die.

Says the booklet, "Wind-thrown trees and logging residuals (are) prime habitat for beetle populations."

Some foresters will read that last sentence and say, "Yep. Wind-thrown trees. That explains it."

I groan inwardly when I'm forced to admit that it's people (*Parasitus worldwidis*) who are culpable. It's hard to admit because I'm one of the biggest culprits.

When I built our homestead, I ended up dropping close to a hundred spruce. I was responsible enough to range the length and breadth of this ridge to take what I could of the dead, dying, and snow-load-cracked trees. I used the trunks for the walls and the tapering tops for rafters and joists. I even carted the branches out of the woods to use as fuel.

But I left many wrong-sized upper parts of the trees where they lay because I had it in my head that deadfall was natural. (Feed the soil! *Opaa!* More grapes for whatever fungi or beetles might live here!)

That was ignorant.

I remember wandering the ridgeline after finishing the house to come upon those "logging residuals" with fondness. What a good manager of resources I was!

And now the lovely tall grove of fifteen spruce right beside the house are struggling with beetle infestation. The largest tree has already become wind-thrown. Its bark, where it lay, showed the unmistakable evidence of spruce beetle attack:

a reddish-brown dust accumulated at the hole bored into the bark, a thin rivulet of pitch. The needles were discolored, as if from lack of water.

The reason that tree died and the others are fighting for their lives is not because of the cyclical nature of forest winnowing and regeneration. It's because I was stupid.

If I had known better—if I had bothered to find out—I would have removed all the trees I cut from where they fell. I would have covered those tree tops too difficult to transport with sheet plastic in order to concentrate the sun's heat, killing the beetle larvae.

The adult beetle is only ¼-inch long, glossy back and segmented into two distinct halves like a rounded loaf of bread with a crease near the middle. The larval stage looks like a tiny white legless grub, suitable for grinding beneath the heel of a boot. The adults are readily squashed, too, but they don't hang around for long after emerging from their bark-burrowed pupae until plunging into a new tree.

The Alaska Department of Natural Resources confirms that in the last few years the beetles have moved into the Susitna Valley.

They don't fly like locusts, ravaging everything in their path. They don't spread by loitering on old toilet seats.

They need, in order to grow in population to epidemic populations, the carelessly ignored deadfall that comes from small scale logging, firewood gathering, cabin building. Windthrown trees are nice, but dumb people are even better.

ΛΛΛ

The patterns of life in the boreal forest are so distinct from human patterns that it's hard not to feel…well, dumb…but also perplexed by how intricate those natural patterns are.

First there was the terrified loon running up the creek.

Not flying or swimming. Running on the unexpected ice against which it beat its wings trying in vain to take flight.

The loon was immature, a gray tuft on its crown instead of an adult's sleek black. But it was almost full-sized, and it had no open water from which to lift itself into the air.

The sudden winter that arrived in mid-September must have frozen a stretch of water during the night where the loon had stopped to feed.

I chased the loon by cutting across the fallen brown grasses between creek oxbows. A few days earlier I had heard of friends in Talkeetna trying to rescue a loon in a similar predicament from an iced-over lake. They'd hoped to catch it in a long-handled salmon net, transport it to open water, and let it free.

All I succeeded in doing by trying to catch the loon on the creek was to terrorize it further. I couldn't step on the thin ice. Maybe it would follow the creek far enough to find another stretch of open water. Probably a fox would leap from the bank to feast in gratitude.

Then there was the bat in the sauna.

As I sat watching the thermometer climb I heard something in the log rafters right overhead. The sound wasn't a rasp or a squeak but plainly the message was one of distress.

Two feet from my face, startled from a few-day-old hibernation, was a brown bat. It tossed its head like a wounded lion, revealing sharply pointed white teeth. It rubbed its face with its "hands" (actually its elbows where its wings bent back), as if trying to block the heat.

My first thought was, "Now what am I going to do with *him?*"

My second thought was, "Hey! What am I going to do with *me?*" I was naked in a very small room with a sharp-toothed bat ready to go mad.

His pain seemed greater than my fear, so I grabbed a cotton glove that I use to lift the water pan from the stove top. I put in on and grasped the bat. It didn't struggle. Then, as I started outside, I thought again. In a sauna, three thoughts in a row was such a strain that I couldn't imagine what to do after

I'd decided that simply tossing the bat into the cold was as much a death sentence as the sauna heat.

But holding a bat with a thin cotton glove seemed dim, too. So I put the bat on the cool floor, furiously repeating, "Hmm, let's see now. Uh..."

It revived and began flying wildly around.

That made things easier, because there was no way I was going to move a muscle.

It alighted again on a rafter. Again I picked it up and ran for the house to climb a ladder leading to the roof. I wanted to slip it into the insulation. It chewed on the glove, which didn't strike me as a sign of thanks.

As soon as I'd put it through a crack beneath the roof boards it squeezed out and flew off.

In the summer, when song birds dart everywhere, we tape cut-out silhouettes of raptors to the windows so smaller birds don't streak headfirst into the glass. A hawk's image keeps its prey from breaking their necks. That's a definite way to "help" the animals that live around us.

Other attempts at virtue are more complicated, because the world is.

⋀⋀⋀ BEARS

Thirty people have been killed by bears in Alaska since 1906. Forty-four people have been killed by domestic dogs in Alaska since 1975.

Bears are not predators that stalk us for food, like tigers. Bears are simply stronger, more self-sufficient, less confrontational, greatly more introspective (half the year fasting and breathing slowly in conscious silence), and twenty million years more evolved. Bears are the representatives on earth that we'd like to be. And so, because it is natural for us to be annoyed by anything that makes us feel ludicrous, we've systematically exterminated them.

One of the last ecosystems where bear populations have not been decimated is this valley. Of course, now that we've arrived in increasing numbers, their population has been reduced.

Still, the valley is large enough for a bear to grow up without any human contact. It's possible for a three-year-old grizzly to look up from its browse to stand face to face with an unfamiliar but colorfully arrayed biped whimpering and flailing the air as it stumbles back or fumbles for a weapon.

In the early 1990s the number of accidental and fatal encounters in Alaska between humans and bears exploded from a historical average of two per summer to fifteen. The number remains at the high end now. Note, though, that the *bears* were the fatalities, the victims, the corpses.

There are about 250 grizzly bears in Denali National Park. No base-line study has ever been done for the griz population in the Su Valley part of the park. The bears here, when they cross outside the invisible boundary of the national park, are fair game. The all-purpose permit to take brown bears is called "defense of life or property."

Our only neighbors, three miles away, who moved years ago, once organized a posse to track a bear that had been in the area of their home. "It could attack our dog lot any time," was the excuse.

I believe that it's genetically impossible for any person to be completely without apprehension about bears, especially in thick brush, unarmed, with bear scat evident. There's always bear scat on our trail in the summer—sometimes just a few piles, sometimes many piles.

Certainly it's work to keep attentive, to make noise so the bears can hear us and avoid confrontation.

But without the presence of bears this world would not be wild.

⋀⋀⋀

"I was just reading an Alaska bear story book," wrote a friend who wants to visit from Boston, "and came away quite sobered." The next three pages of the letter ask, implicitly and imploringly, "So what are the chances that I'm gonna get et?"

The only accurate answer is, of course, "Who knows?"

The chances of being eaten by a bear are a lot less than being struck by lightning while putting for a birdie on the 16th hole of any course anywhere. But it could happen.

Everyone I know who lives in the rural parts of the valley has at least one bear story. The more one gets out and around the back country, the more stories one has.

Here's a typical story, true and unembellished: I was walking quietly on the trail when suddenly a huge griz stood up on its hind legs ten yards away. I stopped. It dropped to all fours and crashed through an alder grove to get away. The end.

Here's another: In April I was traveling by dogsled in the mountains. I was carrying 100 pounds of meat and fat as dog food. Near the top of a narrow glacial canyon, surrounded on three sides by snow peaks, a newly awakened bear stomped toward us atop the crusted snow. The dogs went crazy, barking and bristling and trying to attack. I threw the sled on its side and sat on it so they couldn't go. The bear, stupefied, shook its head repeatedly, annoyed or confused or just unwilling to face a hassle so soon after getting out of bed. Then it climbed a flanking slope, crossed high above us, and kept plowing out toward the valley floor.

For every one time there's a bear "encounter" there are 300 times the bear is aware of us but avoids any contact. I read this fact in a report of some bear biologist, and I believe it, even if the biologist did just guess at that number.

Yet even a fleeting and uneventful meeting with a bear makes for a heart-pounding and knee-weakening reaction. When a friend told me one of his stories about being knocked down by a grizzly's breath (very close encounter, slavering bear, no harm done on either side) I could smell the bear's breath, too, and sense the heat of its proximity, and feel my knees wobble.

When my Boston visitor arrives he'll be lucky if he sees a

bear up close in the woods. He'd never agree that encountering a bear is fortuitous, until after the scare. Then, seeing that he didn't get et, he'll repeat his story, with growing embellishments, until the day he dies.

ᴧᴧᴧ

I'd just bent over to pick a translucent orange cloudberry on the tundra when a brown bear burst from treeline fifty yards away.

I carried no gun. We often go out on the tundra to swim in the lake or romp with the dogs or pick berries. Constantly lugging a shotgun around the backyard is too much a burden for daily life.

But here was the one-in-a-million chance. The bear came straight at me. Its mouth was open. A dark red wound covered one shoulder. There was no tree to climb, nowhere to hide.

The last thing I remember is chuckling, because I was in bed dreaming. And in my dream I had A Secret Weapon.

My confidence is contained in an aerosol can seven inches tall and two inches wide. The little spray can is filled with propellant and *oleoresin capsicum*, which is Latin for cayenne pepper. Very hot cayenne pepper. Eye-blinding, nose-burning, tongue-numbing cayenne pepper.

Imagine a bear, which has one of the most sensitive noses of any creature, snorting a big draught of cayenne snuff, gasping for breath, rubbing needles from its eyes. And then, a few hours later, when the pain has disappeared, imagine the bear still alive, not pumped full of magnum slugs or, worse, wounded by magnum slugs.

This pepper spray is sold in gun shops in Alaska, in drugstores, in supermarkets. Some people maintain that it would do little more to a charging bear than nicely spice its meal. But I know many people who have used it in close encounters, and it's worked.

It's changed, for us, the nature of being in the wild. Even carrying a large gun makes me leery of bear encounters because using the gun means death or maiming. With the spray we can watch game without needing to immediately slink away for fear of closer contact.

I have no doubt that a can of bear repellent has its limitations. One can marinate in the strongest bug repellent and still get bit. When I used the pepper spray on a fight between our two most aggressive male dogs they did stop ripping each other, but it took a few seconds for their bloodlust to cool. In those few seconds a bear in equal rage could remove two or three helplessly flailing limbs before taking a breath.

But the mythology of bears is such that nothing short of a bazooka is going to stop a charging bear cold. Bears have digested a magazine of bullets before slowing down.

Any weapon in the woods carried for protection is an assumption of faith. Guns misfire. And *every* weapon needs to be aimed accurately before it can work. We use the cayenne less to strut with a feeling of power than to have something to bolster our faith.

When our boys go down to the creek to fish or out on the tundra to swim they carry the spray. It gives them a sense of security. They feel overwhelmed by the prospect of carrying the big shotgun or similar large-bore rifle. Few kids, unlike adults, are adept at masking fear. Acting macho is an acquired trait.

When the older boys go off alone on a six-day backpacking trip into the hills, eagerly, I'm glad for the little can strapped on one of their belts. It has helped them investigate the nature of the wild.

KIDS IN
THE WOODS

Kids often know what's vital because they see what they see and feel what they feel and do what they do without any intermediate step like rational analysis, which at times can be a problem. ("What are you *doing*?" is a common parental cry of disbelief. "Just pouring this juice on the rug," is a typical stupefyingly simple and honest kid reply.) The problem, however, usually belongs to the adults, who more often than not have lost interest in the manifold possibilities of the world.

That's why I trust kids' perceptions. The purity of what they see isn't filtered by preconceptions. There's too much new going on all the time to stayed bored. In the absence of boredom is insight into what matters.

Everything matters.

Just look!

Kids, by definition, are *sui generis*. They haven't a clue what the world has been nor what it could conceivably be with the right artistic vision rendered laboriously. The world just is. Alluring or redundant. Way cool or real dumb.

I am grateful for and humbled by the kids here who live with one foot in the Pleistocene and one foot in Air Jordans. They're growing up with the unending world of snow peaks and the ephemeral intrigue of Nintendo. They live with both the dreamy serenity of Huck Finn's river trips and the sudden shock of F-15s. As is particularly common in very rural areas, there is incest and abuse and suicide, poverty and bigotry. Life's not a summer idyll. No child escapes his or her family pretty much ever, certainly not by moving with them to or growing up in a distant place.

I don't want to pretend that the kids' perceptions are always more astute than those of their parents. A child's world is often so hidden, because verbal capacity is lacking, that much of what we see in them is just what we *can* see, from our distant perspective.

But what they reveal about this landscape is critical to note, not just because they see it without association but because they will determine how it becomes seen—as constant or mutable, as worthy of maintaining or necessary to develop, as a home to honor or just some boondock to get out of fast into the "real" world.

/\\/\\/\\

"Him dead, Dod?"

We were poking at the carcass of a beaver, its back ripped open, the only tracks surrounding it on the soft spring snow ours, father and then-three-year-old firstborn son. The beaver had been trying to reach the woods still ten yards from where it lay. The frozen tundra lake from which it had come had not yet begun to thaw.

"Him dead like the salmon in the creek?"

The previous fall salmon had flung themselves from the creek after spawning, lying atop the bank, eyes filmed over, bodies stiff.

The beaver, obviously in search of food, had crawled atop the snow from a hole clawed in the lingering lake ice. But there was no predator track around it, no bear, no wolverine, no fox, no wolf. The blood was still fresh on its back.

That beaver didn't die from a lightning bolt. It didn't die from gunshot, both evidently—only violent claw or fang could have caused such a wound—and circumstantially: there are no other people anywhere near where we live. An animal killed it. Or something like an animal. But how?

I was spooked.

The child was fascinated.

All those European "fairy" tales of monsters and beasts and demons and witches in the woods that remain inexcusably a part of our cultural upbringing came back to haunt me. I glanced around, warily.

My son poked at the head with a firm finger like an examining zoologist.

"Him really, really dead?" he asked, double checking the undoubtable simply to have it confirmed, since, in the truly wondrous world of children, miracle is as possible as anything.

Then an enormous bald eagle lifted off from a spruce nearby. Its wing beat was barely audible, an intake of breath, a sigh. It flapped overhead, caught a thermal off the radiant snow, and began soaring.

We both stared, mouths open.

"That beaver is really, really dead," I said. "Because that eagle saw him walking on the snow and came down silently from the sky *wwwhhop!* on his back and ripped him apart."

The effect of my melodramatic interpretation of reality didn't produce a dramatic reaction. He turned from the sky to study the splayed body, dispassionately. The truth of what my boy saw was what it was. Eagle, beaver, life, death. Nothing more or less. Not even an excitable dad's storyline compelled him into thrill or terror.

Was he impressed? Deeply. He stood up to look at the

eagle's spiralling ascent, squatted back next to the beaver, touched its back, stroked its glistening fur.

Did he come to fear eagles or open spring tundra? Not at all, though he was prudent enough to ask if eagles ever killed people. ("Never," firmly, conclusively.)

Did he have nightmares about sudden violent death? It was *I* who rendered the natural process of life in terms of horror. And he didn't buy it.

When my father died, the only grandpa this boy has ever known, his question was the same: "Him really, really dead?"

I tried to answer in florid explanations of the continuity of love and the unending sustenance of connection.

Janus, who was named for the Roman god of beginnings and endings, suffered my expansiveness patiently. He already knew that stuff.

His grandpa was really, really dead, and it was part of life.

ʌʌʌ

"Saint Francis was not a lover of nature," wrote G.K. Chesterton in his biography of Francis. To Chesterton, the phrase "lover of nature" implied a "sort of sentimental pantheism" in which the natural world is simply a pleasant background.

But for Francis, "nothing was ever in the background.... He saw everything as dramatic, distinct from its setting, not all of a piece like a picture, but in action like a play. A bird went by him like an arrow.... A bush could stop him like a brigand."

I'd thought of that most childlike of saints when Janus, at age four, spotted a gray jay through the window, ran for his boots, grabbed a handful of dog food, and went outside to stand utterly still, hand extended, food in his palm, eyes on the food, waiting for the flutter of air over his shoulder to alight on his wrist.

To be outside with an alert kid is to be forced into constant awareness. "Look at this moss!" "Feel this mushroom!" "What bird is that behind the tree?" "Did the mouse make this hole to come up out of the snow or go down in?" "Quiet! I hear something!"

Living deep in the forest makes it impossible for there to be background because we're as far back and as close to the ground as can be. And at four everything is action and drama. "Drama," in my 1926 Webster's, is "a series of real events invested with unity and interest." That seems a pretty good way to see the world. And it isn't melodrama, which requires exaggeration.

It's also a pretty demanding way to live. A saint might be focussed solely on the vitality of the world, and a child might be constantly vital, but the rest of us have to work at it.

Gary Snyder, a poet and amateur anthropologist, has said, "Our earlier traditions of life prior to agriculture required literally thousands of years of great attention and awareness, and long hours of stillness."

The manner by which *Homo sapiens* flourished was not only by technology (spears and sharpened rocks, bows and guns and computers) but by our ability to observe. In those thousands of years of unsentimental observation we came to understand the natural world so intimately that we could trust the patterns of wild game and wind, knowing, of course, that the trust required faith.

Because we looked, we saw the world in its multiple dimensions: the intricate course of game across migratory distance, the depth of roots, the height of storm clouds. And we saw the world within the swirls and loops of time. Most of us tend to view time as linear—point to point, goal to goal. The stars can be seen to follow a steady predictable progression through the night sky or they can whirl in such astronomical complexity that to see their possibilities is to be struck dumb, in stillness.

Once, with Janus, before he had brothers, we returned on our trail from the road to spot a flock of about thirty trumpeter swans on our largest tundra lake. We'd never seen so many so close before. We crept closer. When they sensed our insistent intrusion they took flight. We chased, but they disappeared just above the trees.

Then, in an unexpected loop, the entire flock returned in formation no more than twenty feet directly overhead, honking and swivelling their heads to nod. It was wondrous drama.

"Will they live here?" whispered the child when he finally broke his stillness. I said they might return again next year if they liked us.

The birds went by like an arrow, and he was stopped in his tracks.

/\\.\\/\\

Got him.

Or her.

"If it's a her will the babies still be left up in the insulation?" asked the boy.

"It's too early in the year for squirrels to have babies," I said. "This squirrel only left 10,000 pine cones up in the insulation."

We'd watched it for days make a nest in the ceiling, carrying pine cones in, tossing fiberglass out, leaving the smell of urine above the bed where we slept, getting bolder and bolder in its familiarity with our house. I assumed I'd just shoot it since inevitably it would ransack the house. But I worried that my kid's last words before they led him away would be, "But what's *wrong* with killing things that get in your way?"

So here's what we did: First we took the long journey to Anchorage's animal shelter to get a live trap—a cage with a trip-wire door to catch but not hurt the squirrel. The shelter is an airy modern building with high ceilings and tiled walls. It reminded me of a crematorium I once saw in Los Angeles. The shelter holds stray cats and dogs for three days, then gasses them.

But the people who work there are genuinely compassionate about animals.

"Blow the squirrel's head off with a shotgun?" they gasped

when I'd mentioned my alternative to a live trap.

"Well, it's just a figure of speech," I said.

"That's awful!"

"It's what I'm trying to avoid."

But they had no live traps available. All were on loan. There was a long waiting list.

That intrigued me. I view Anchorage as a decidedly urban environment. Suddenly I had to consider how close the city's electric gridwork really is to the natural world. How unusual to imagine that a conscientious citizenry benevolently removes strayed muskrats and snowshoe hares and lynx and fox back to the wild.

"What do people set for here in town?" I asked.

"Just house cats," was the reply.

The woman in charge leaned over a counter to whisper, "Why not just poison the squirrel? It's so much more humane than shooting it."

At that moment my son came racing in from the room where the dogs are penned. "I found three I really like!" he announced. "Can we take them?"

"More dogs are the last thing we need," I said.

"You said a squirrel in the house is the last thing we need," he countered.

When we got home the next day the squirrel greeted us with its raucous bray as if to brag about how much more damage it did to the insulation.

That night, lying awake listening to rodent teeth chew, I thought of a plan.

In the morning we strung a rope between two trees and hung a pulley. Under the pulley, upside down, held off the ground by a line passed through holes punched in its bottom, we hung a thirty-two-gallon aluminum garbage can. The line from the can through the pulley stretched into the house. Under the can we laid a piece of plywood with almonds and peanut butter dead center.

Then we waited. Our trap looked ridiculous: a lynched

garbage can. The boy didn't care. He sat at the window for hours watching the squirrel ignore our set to carry more pine cones up the outside wall into the eaves.

Two days later we got him. Or her.

"He's eating the bait!" the watchful boy cried. "He's right here!"

I loosed the line and the can rang down. The dogs started barking. We ran outside.

"We got him! We got him! Let's feed him to the dogs!" shouted the boy.

I said that we were trying to avoid killing it.

"Then let's keep him for a pet! He can live inside the house!"

We slipped a lid under the trap, strapped the assembly tight, and loaded it in the dogsled. A mile away, under a tall spruce that had lots of pine cones, we let the squirrel go. I took a snapshot of the World's Best Squirrel Trapper standing beside his garbage can beaming with pride and the pleasure of mercy.

"Home range is 500 to 600 feet across, and the squirrel seldom leaves his area," says our *Alaska Mammals* reference book.

Three days passed. At six a.m. the sleep-defying cry from the porch railing outside the bedroom window announced the first squirrel's return from The Far Horizon, a three-day journey past fox and owl and marten. Then it scampered up to the insulation and began gnawing.

So here's our "Lady or the Tiger" dilemma. Behind one door is a shotgun. Behind a second is an upside-down garbage can. Behind the third door is a squirrel for a "pet."

We have to choose.

ᴧᴧ

Do children raised in remote areas end up in Los Angeles intoxicated by shopping malls and drive-thru diners? Will they come to dream of seventy-two-channel television and video arcades?

I've considered this possibility with the smallest twinge of concern. Maybe we should send our boys to summer camp in a church basement in downtown Chicago the way urban parents try to send their kids to Camp Waybackinwoods. Maybe a satellite dish and generator is a good way to spend a winter's night instead of watching moonshadows. After all, I grew up with The Three Stooges and the Mickey Mouse Club and dreamed of the forest.

Lately, however, I've found a better answer. Spruce bonfires.

Not cottonwood bonfires, which hiss, or birch bonfires, which smoke. Spruce. Dead dried gray solid spruce with kindling of spruce branches. That kind of bonfire crackles and leaps and roars. It makes great flaring shapes of flame. It lights up the night like a neon carnival.

Twice so far this winter I've taken my youngest son out on the dogsled for camping trips into the Alaska Range. We picked warmish days, loaded up with carob chips and raisins, spread a down sleeping bag in the sled basket, and headed for the hills.

Long runs with the dogs are common for a kid who has no alternative transportation into or out from his home. He sees the mountains out the front window the way a city kid sees the buildings across the street. It's common to take for granted that which is common.

But spruce bonfires are like fireworks: a celebration.

The first night out we stopped at treeline in the Peters Hills, between two great glaciers. While I unharnessed the dogs I got complaints about cold hands. While I piled branches for the fire the complaints were about hunger, "and not for no more raisins." But then when I lit the tinder and the blue snowscape became an orange rocket launching pad, nothing else mattered.

Snow mountains may create awe, the winter forest serenity, but a blazing spruce fire is a festival of light.

For hours young Prometheus tended his fire, sticking it with a stick, stomping embers, prancing round and round the shadow and glow. He helped cook by tossing snow into the pot balanced atop coals, missing more often than hitting, which created steam and hiss, which was the idea. "I like being in the mountains!" he kept crying, though the mountains were invisible behind the circle of light.

Finally I showed him how much fun it was to kick lots of snow into the flames. When the steam subsided and the stars returned I had to promise an even bigger bonfire the next night before he'd crawl with me into the tent.

The next morning we stopped often to hack down small dead swamp spruce and toss them in the front of the sled. "There! Go up there! I see another one!" That night was as exciting as the first with the same exhilaration and the same letdown when the fire was gone.

When we arrived back home the following night it took a lot of convincing before we could build a spruce bonfire in the cookstove and not outside.

I no longer worry that someday I'll get a postcard from West Hollywood telling me that the highest happiness is shopping on Rodeo Drive. I worry that I'll have to lug a dead swamp spruce up Denali when it comes time to show the boys the summit.

ΛΛΛ

The 7,250 foot level of the Southeast Fork of the Kahiltna Glacier is Base Camp for Denali climbs. Mount Hunter (Denali's Son), jagged and avalanche-swept, is less than a mile away across the ice river of the Southeast Fork. Mount Foraker (Denali's Wife), twice as imposing, buttresses the far side of the Kahiltna. Denali itself, the third leg of the triangle, looms like a thunderhead.

To be amidst it all is like being in the heart of the Great Pyramid of Cheops, like being in the throne room of the Potala, like entering Dante's ninth ring of heaven.

For the first time in his life, our six-year-old uses his favorite word accurately. "Awesome," he whispers. "Look how blue the ice is."

That's what I want to hear. That's the reason for taking the kids up here in the same ski-equipped bush planes that transport serious climbers.

"Now pull me the rest of the way up the hill."

That's not what I want to hear. That's the reason for waiting a few more years for taking the kids further up the mountain.

"Just think," says our eight-year-old. "People come from all over the world just to be here. Right here," stamping his foot on the snow. "Now I see why."

Atta boy. That's the right perspective.

"But I won't use these old skis. I want skis like *those*," pointing to a professional climber with thousands of dollars worth of fancy gear. "My skis suck."

Oh boy. Why are we up here with kids?

It's snowing now. We're in a cloud, so the snow drifts around like mist. It's full radiant summer a mile below on the valley floor but the best this elevation can do is offer wet snow rather than dry and cold. This is the dreaded "weather day" when kids whine about being "stuck in the tent."

But there's no whining. There's excitement to finish digging the snow cave and to listen for bass-roaring avalanches and to laugh at funny stories about past mountain adventures.

This is why we're up here with the kids. They love it. It is certainly worthy of the deepest love. And they feel it, deeply.

In the door of a nearby tent, waiting for a bush plane to take them back to Talkeetna, their mountain adventure over, their summit bagged, a couple of climbers in fluorescent Gore-Tex talk loudly of beer. They're annoyed that it's a weather day, with no planes.

I like the way the kids see it.

∧∧∧

It's blinding sun now. In these mountains the weather changes like lightning. I run after the kids shouting to keep their goggles on. The intensity of this light off the ice is like staring at the sun. Without goggles they'll go snowblind, which, though not permanent, is excruciatingly painful and literally blinding.

They ski down a slope (ski, plop, ski, plop, grin) and take their goggles off. The goggles don't fit right. The goggles get clouded with sweat. The goggles are *dumb*.

"I said keep those goggles ON!"

The sun burns into our brains, makes us giddy. It's beautiful and demanding, like love.

"I'm not drinking that water. You melted snow from where my brother pissed."

"How come you pulled him up the hill and not me?"

"I couldn't find the toilet paper so I used your sock."

"I'm not eating that oatmeal. You made it with the piss water."

Arghhh! These children!

It's night now. "Night." The pastel luminescence at one a.m. in these summer mountains colors the slopes, saturates the tent, makes it hard to sleep because sleep would shut out the beauty.

"Just read one more chapter!"

"Let's play *Go Fish!*"

"Tell us more funny stories!"

It's hard to deny enthusiasm. We won't be here long. The hope is to make it so enticing and so comfortable that returning—and going further—will be a joy.

So we read one more chapter and play one more game of cards with the deck we made from scrap paper and two differently colored pens. Then one last story about a professional mountaineer who skied down a steep slope to show his ability, tripped, flipped, and landed on his butt.

In their sleep, the boys continue to smile, at everything.

It snowed during the night but it's clear and bitter cold now.

The six-year-old races from the kids' tent to the adults' tent. His bottom is bare. He snuggles between the adults, sticks his cold feet on my belly, and grins.

"Me and my brother think the Kings are in."

"The what?"

"The Kings! Lots of 'em. Can I use the big salmon pole?"

So when we finally fly out, amidst the ringing light, it's with our sights ahead, toward the fishing holes.

I'd never before left the mountains except longingly, gazing back over my shoulder.

I like the way the kids see it.

⋀⋀⋀

It's past midnight and still the horizon north is flamboyant maroon sunset.

It's night, I say.

My fisherman son ignores me.

It's nighttime, I say.

He responds with a grunt and pokes another salmon egg onto his hook.

It's time to sleep, I say.

I'm a good dad. I announce the hour.

He casts into the creek where the light reflects off the water, where the fish ignore both the bait and the hour.

It's light, he says without looking at me.

It's nighttime, I repeat.

I feel like a fool who holds up an apple and insists, "Orange!"

Nighttime means dark. Nighttime means that the water becomes inky and then just a sound.

He's never known a summer night when the light fades and the fish sleep. He's only known summer nights when dad becomes insistent. That's because dad looks at the clock. If dad didn't look at the clock, he'd fish all night.

In traditional Inuit culture children are never ordered to bed. That's the beauty and difference of Eskimo child rearing. I've watched kids in arctic coastal villages wander around until they drop.

But they don't whine. They don't demand. Their dads don't watch the clock.

Just a few more casts, my son says.

He has no idea what he's just said. It's automatic. If I had told him a meteor was streaking toward his fishing hole he'd keep staring intently at the creek and say, "Just a few more casts."

He's watching the wake of the fish. At this hour the wakes are phosphorescent. The creek itself glows. It echoes the sky.

I get tough. I huff and puff.

Time to go now, I say.

He grins at me. Then he casts. I think of Eskimos.

If he was raised where I was raised, in the great fields of the Republic, he'd sleep. He wouldn't have an excuse. Dark is dark. Night is sleep. My childhood summers were times of long days and deep nights, nights of constellations and fireflies and the drone of freight trains in the distance. Lying down was communion with the mysteries of night, listening to long silences, watching stars, dreaming. Everywhere was night.

The whole world's sleeping, I say.

He just grunts. He knows it's a lie.

In our world little is at rest. Plants still grow. Bears forage. Salmon swim. This latitude gets as much sunlight in a year as the tropics, but it gets it in a rush. Life makes the most of it.

Biologists call the northern animals that don't keep to a fixed twenty-four-hour internal clock "free ranging." They keep going until they drop. They'll catch up on sleep later. The best example of a free ranging animal is a six-year-old boy.

"A big one! I see a big one! Quick! Hand me the bait!"

Most people live by definite internal clocks. That's why jet lag is a real phenomenon. But most of us in the far north stay up "late" in the summer and go to bed "early" in the winter. One of the sacred codes by which kids live is to never admit being tired. In the northern summer, especially when the fish are running, it's easy to ignore all pretext of schedule.

Just a few more casts.

When I finally corral him and carry him, reeking of fish, to the tent, he's asleep before I can nestle him in the bag.

In the distance, a salmon jumps.

/\/\/\

Camping with kids is like foreign travel with a native interpreter. Much is revealed. Your prejudices are exposed. The pride you take in your discerning eye and critical judgment is shown to be a lot of hooey. Much more is going on than you'd ever see on your own.

It's embarrassing to stand calculating the way back to camp until deciding, based on the angle of the sun, "This way," only to have a kid who's been looking down for neat rocks all day announce, "I'm taking a shortcut!" and beat you back.

I've found it common to discover an unusual plant or mushroom, point it out, and have the offhand response of a kid be, "Yeah, there's a whole bunch of them over there."

I figure the reason they see so much is because they're low to the ground.

As an adult, I have a specific routine for sleeping in a tent, especially when it's cold. Years of trial and error have made me competent. I shared my knowledge with the boys: Wear a hat because much body heat is lost through the head. Don't extend feet or arms off the ground pad because the insulating quality will be lost. Stay close together. Make a pillow from your coat.

In the morning both were bareheaded, in opposite corners of the tent, at ninety degrees to the pads, and well rested. I was tired from having awakened a few times to move them into "proper" positions.

We spend a lot of time camping, though not much in "campgrounds." There are none in this valley's back country. Along the truncated road system the designated camping sites are usually filled with Winnebagos. When we do fill out the duplicate forms required for a numbered spot in an official camping area the boys are glad. It's almost as cool as staying in a motel.

Their favorite campgrounds by far are those of Denali National Park. Every year we drive over the Range and into the hubbub of Alaska's biggest tourist attraction. It's like going to the circus. There are strange people from faraway countries, wild animals so used to the activity that they can be seen up close, and amazing virtuoso Winnebago acts.

After we get our permit and set up our tent the kids walk around watching the Winnebagos. I could care less. The kids are enthralled. Some are as elaborate as touring buses for rock stars. Some have as much glass as fancy railroad dome cars. Some disgorge people like clowns from small cars in the center ring.

The Winnebagos outnumber the tents ten to one. Even when a screened porch is unrolled from a rooftop, spread with Astroturf, and set up with comfortable reclining chairs, the "campers" still go back inside their metal box to sleep. The kids love that. It's unfathomable.

Camping to them is exploration. Even in a campground they find peripheral places more frequented by animals (squirrels, grey jays, magpies, lemmings) than people. They discover dead wood for the fire even though logic would suggest that the area should have been picked clean years ago.

In the back country, by winter dogsled or summer hike, mysterious tracks or old bones or a moose rack turn up with a frequency that keeps them attentive. I am often intent upon getting somewhere. I try to cover a certain preconceived distance to make it to a creek for water or to stay on schedule for the amount of food we're carrying. I have an entire Winnebago of stuff in my head. They just look at what's interesting.

I justify our different foci by pretending that I'm the one concentrating on what's important. But they know that nothing really matters when exploring other than discovery.

ᛗᛗ

White Arrow, at age ten, slept outside alone last night. He had no tent, the temperature was thirty-eight, the drizzle was steady, a breeze was blowing.

White Arrow chose his name himself when he was about eight. His younger brother, Catching Spear, became who he is, rather than what his parents originally decided, at the same time. If ever mother or father call them by their birth-certificate names they'll ignore us utterly, not even bothering with annoyance or contempt. Their baby brother was named Forrest, which seemed acceptable without revision.

The bigger boys make their own bows, hunt without supervision, and make secret trails that lead to secret blinds. What they consider their "real" names are in keeping with what they consider their real world.

White Arrow for six months had been harboring the fantasy of spending a night alone in the forest with only his knife. I'm not sure where he got the idea, but it's such a pervasive human desire that he probably picked it up from the same unconscious place he got his name. The desire to test one's capacity, to survive with no support other than one's own strength, to find confidence in frightening situations—that seems both a male and female rite of passage, though plainly the boy's method is very much a man's approach.

The common cultural manifestation of that impulse now is to go away to college—without mommy or daddy!—alone and independent.

But White Arrow decided to test his competence at age ten.

It might have been because I'm so relentless in my criticism of particular news items that reach us on our radio. When another twin-rotor National Guard helicopter has to rescue an injured climber on Denali I say something like, "There's another bozo who didn't know how to dig a snow cave." When hunters get lost for days and require state troopers with dogs to find them, I bring out a map and compass and become didactic. When villagers in the Yukon-Kuskokwim Delta fall out of their boats and drown I point out that a life jacket would have saved them.

I try to indoctrinate competence.

But the immediate impetus for White Arrow's decision was our reading aloud a novel about Geronimo, *Watch for Men on the Mountain*. The book portrays the staggering capacity for survival of the Apache as they fled from the white man's cavalry in order to live where they wished—in the forests and mountains. Men, women, and children in their constant flight would sleep without even a blanket for warmth.

The next night the boy put on his pile pants, wool socks and hat, and announced that he'd be gone until morning.

I suggested that he also take an old Army surplus rain poncho and a foam pad to keep the rain off him and from beneath him.

I didn't doubt that he was serious. I only wanted him to survive without pneumonia.

The creek was already flooded. Our trail to the road was a river.

He marched out, resolute, at 9:30, in the dark of a late September. I gave him an hour. I was glad that he wanted to try.

After an hour (I was watching the clock), with the dogs huddled silently in their houses having failed to announce anyone's return, I put on my rain gear and went outside to find him.

I couldn't find him.

A half-hour later I returned to the house. I refused to worry.

I worried. A bear! Hypothermia! Dazed wandering in the black night unable to find the house!

I quelled my fears by sticking in earplugs and lying under the bedcovers. This was his test, and a dad stomping around with a flashlight crying, "Yoo-hoo! Where are you, darling?" would blow everything. His mother had an intuitive trust *I* lacked.

I drifted to sleep and woke a few hours later, completely baffled how he could have lasted so long in the weather with such paltry gear. One explanation was that he was dead. Before I again went outside I checked upstairs.

His down sleeping bag was full. To make sure, I touched the bottom and gently squeezed a foot. Then I sneaked back to bed.

In the morning he was exultant. "I stayed out until five a.m." he announced, though he admitted that he didn't look at a clock.

I didn't quibble. He had tested his ability against bears and bogeymen and hypothermia and fear.

It seemed obvious to me that this was just the first of many such expeditions, each one a little further afield. It also seemed plain that his tests will become mine, too. I won't be learning to trust in my competence. I'll be learning to trust in his.

ᴧᴧᴧ

"That's glacier dust," I called, pointing to a wall ten yards away.

Catching Spear snowplowed to a stop beside me. He pushed up his ski goggles and squinted. "Cool," he said, non-committally.

"It doesn't look like much," I admitted.

We'd come up Hidden River to ascend the Buckskin Glacier, his turn for a solo trip with his father. We'd explored a waterfall completely encased in a long fluted tube of ice created by its own spray. We'd seen fifteen ptarmigan, five moose, three porcupines, and a wolverine. We'd been traveling for three days in high style: the boy on skis towed like a water skier behind the dogsled that moved swiftly in what had been great conditions.

Comparatively, the three-foot-tall strip of grey revealed by an undulation in the glacier looked incidental.

The dogs, tired from the day's thirty-mile run, lay in the snow. I took an ice axe from the sled and we walked over to the wall. When we touched it where it baked in the sun what had appeared solid crumbled into a rivulet of fine powder.

"Hey, it *is* glacier dust! Mom's gonna be happy," said the boy.

In addition to exploring a part of the range we hadn't yet been, we were hoping to bring back some of the pulverized rock of mountains that the glacier had carried down from the heights and ground to dust. It's great for the garden.

He played avalanche games by poking the wall with the axe. Then suddenly he fell to his knees and whispered, "Dad. Wait."

He took off a glove and picked up a handful of dust, letting it slowly trickle through his fingers.

With uncharacteristic gravity he turned to look at me. Quietly he said, "Dad, I think there's gold here."

I stooped beside him. There was a vein of very evident gold-colored flecks in the gray. "Well it's possible," I said. "Though it's probably just pyrite."

"No, look!" he said, getting excited. "This is...this is *gold!*"

From what little I knew, it seemed unlikely. But once in Chicago on a visit to Grandma, when the boy was four, we were strolling along Lake Michigan's concrete breakwater when he pointed to a big white bird sitting atop a "No Swimming" sign. "Snowy owl," he said, casually. I smiled and dutifully explained that Chicago had big sea gulls, certainly not boreal raptors. Then the snowy owl lifted itself from its perch with a powerful wing stroke. "See?" said the boy matter-of-factly while I stared.

So I'd learned early not to discount his perceptions.

Besides, what if it was gold?

Suddenly the scene crystallized. I saw him as he was at eleven years old, his face alight with wonder, his hand outstretched, fingers slightly curled as if in supplication, the brilliant snowfield muted only by the crease of slate gray that steadily, as I stared, began to glitter.

I ran for the sled to get a bag.

That evening, as we sat around camp, we talked a lot of gold. We would make hauls with the dogs from the vein to a flat stretch further downriver where a small plane would load it. We'd only tell our best friends where we found it. We'd buy an

RC-10 remote-controlled hobby car. Living near gold country in Alaska makes it hard not to talk of gold, just as talk of bears and mountains keeps recurring.

Before we went to sleep we chose names for the peaks surrounding us, since there were none on the map. I studied those peaks also to know exactly where to return.

When we finally came out from the land and reached home, Catching Spear grabbed a plate while I was unloading gear. He panned the flakes from the dust as best he could and put a sampling in a jar. Our plan was to go see Bob Young in Talkeetna the next day, one of the area's real miners.

Bob, in a Caterpillar Tractor billed cap and khaki work uniform, stopped tinkering with a motor when we arrived. He has a grandson my boy's age. He grinned when he saw the jar. "Well let's see what we've got here," he said.

He led us to a large shed filled with mining tools to find a pan, then back out into the spring sunlight where he scooped up some melt water and set to work, swirling the contents of the jar deftly in the pan, tipping out bits of muddied water.

"It sure could have some gold in it," he said helpfully.

The boy held his breath.

"But it looks like what you've got is just mica. It's not pyrite. The dust is probably quartz."

Catching Spear was crestfallen.

Bob noticed. "Wait now and I'll show you pyrite." He went back to the shed. He put a handful of gravel from a five-gallon bucket into the pan.

When he'd panned off some of it he poked around with a finger and held up a piece of pyrite to show us how it differed from mica. The boy was polite, but distracted.

"Oh, and what've we got here?" Bob added, picking out a little nugget. "This is gold. See how it's the same color all around? Here, son, you keep it. Then you'll know what gold looks like, too."

The boy lit up as if he'd just found the motherlode.

That small nugget now sits above his bed, in its own jar.

Later that day I overheard a local climber ask him what liked best about being up the Buckskin, a very rarely visited part of the Range. "Almost finding gold," was the reply. Then, with a sudden spark, "And seeing a wolverine."

∿∿∿

Much of the kids' play in the woods is inventive. "Monopoly" and "Scrabble" and even a little battery-operated handheld video game, all of which we store under a couch, are rarely played. What they do to entertain themselves, especially as they get older, is to make stuff up.

"What do your kids do all day?" is a common question from curious adults so utterly lacking in imagination that they have to ask.

In the house we now have a batting cage. A tennis ball was punctured through the middle by a heated cabin spike, an eighth-inch-thick line pushed completely through, tied off, and hung from a ceiling rafter, suspended at waist-height. The line is just short enough so that the ball will not, when struck, arc into anything other than the ceiling or the door. When kid friends visit, they take their turn hitting the ball with a bat or pretending it's an Evil Ninja to be kick-boxed. ("If you miss and it touches you you're dead.") They all seem to assume that it's as common a toy as blocks.

Outside, the guys build various designs of rafts to float on the swimming lake. Logs were the material of choice until they discovered that one of the islands, six feet in circumference, that populate the shallow lake could be torn from the bottom. "The Floating Island" now gets poled around the lake, or rowed, or sailed.

The heavily-thorned devil's club plant, closely related to ginseng, became more than a four-foot-tall weed to be slashed with a machete when an herb book revealed that its roots are a tonic. "Used by Alaska Native cultures for general strength...."

The boys dig it up, peel the root bark, grind it in a mortar and pestle, tamp it into gelatin capsules they got from somewhere, and pop "Power Pills."

One of the creations of which they're most proud is the Zoob Tube. They started with a piece of old slingshot rubber tubing. They poked it between logs upstairs in their room so that half was inside and half out. A series of rusted stove pipes and discarded plastic gutter pipes and hacksaw-cut steel gasoline cans carry any liquid poured into the tube out over the porch and roof to drain into grass. "Poured" is not the proper verb. "Pissed" is. Now they don't have to carry their "pee cans" outside to dump after filling them during the night.

The bows they carve from bent alders are necessary weapons to make for every buddy—boy or girl—who visits. The bows are powerful. An arrow shot for distance will disappear from sight. An arrow shot into a target (currently a three-foot-tall stuffed bear won at a ball-throwing booth at the Alaska State Fair) will quiver furiously.

At the end of salmon season a group of kids will go to all the public-access fishing spots. They'll fish for lures. Gleaming on the bottom of the creek will be many snagged lures left behind. If they can't hook them, they'll swim and dive. Their tackle boxes are always full.

I once did a magazine article that required talking with a dozen adults who had been raised in the bush—on homesteads or other remote locations. Some of those "kids" were professionals, some unemployed, one a well-known politician, one a successful songwriter. A few were old enough to have grandchildren. Without exception they agreed that growing up with the woods or mountains surrounding them was the best part of childhood regardless of whether their families were nurturing or abusive.

"I felt connected to something I loved," said the most articulate. "It made everything fun. I felt rich."

∧∨∧

In the front yard we have a three-foot-tall tree stump that weighs a couple of tons and could stop a tank. Every time buddies come to visit the rotting stump gets heavier and more invulnerable.

Almost all boys older than ten in the upper part of this valley have their own .22 rifles.

The stump has so many lead bullets in it that it could sink through the earth to China. I keep hoping it will, just to get rid of it.

By this point the boys' bullets are not being stopped by old wood, but by other bullets. The bullets fuse. A .22 bullet is the size of a small peanut—not the peanut shell, but the nut. We've dug out chunks of lead as big as golf balls.

At first we used the stump to set targets *atop:* cans, an occasional bottle, pieces of cardboard with bull's-eyes drawn on them. After hundreds of rounds it occurred to me, slowly, that the lead was flying off into the forest to poison both the creek and the birds that might swallow the shot for their crops.

So we started placing the targets *against* the stump. Even if the target was not hit, the stump would catch the bullet.

Now we have enough toxic metal in that stump for it to be declared a hazardous waste zone by the EPA.

We also have a small mountain of brass casings. But the casings have (mostly) been collected and put into a canvas bag. That treasure impresses any kid.

A .22 casing, unfortunately, cannot be reloaded.

But these problems are the price paid to become a good shot. The boys can now hit, from twenty paces, a plastic stegosaurus tail, a Walkman foam earphone cover, a withered radish, and, best of all, a dime. Prominently displayed in the boys' room are dimes that look as if they'd been punched in the midsection—doubled over, crumpled up.

By my count these targets became easy to hit about a thousand rounds ago. But, as the boys point out, practice keeps the eye sharp.

For a few years the boys' bang of choice came from fireworks, which are legal in the valley. We probably have as many thin red bamboo bottle rocket sticks as lead bullets scattered around the forest. Fireworks, however, gave way to rifles as soon as the boys were big enough to hold the barrel parallel to the ground.

The one constant is the blam of gunpowder.

Columnist Dave Barry, the poet laureate of male adolescence, astutely observed that a bunch of boys shipwrecked on a deserted island would, before anything else, make pretend guns from appropriately shaped driftwood.

The most I can do in response to this truth is to monitor the shooting sessions with firm rules. They do not put a round in the chamber until they're ready to shoot. They do not get ready to shoot until everyone else is behind the gun. And they never, never pretend that the gun is anything other than a weapon of death, even if what dies is just a dime. If the rifle is pointed at another person—even if unloaded with the chamber open—the rifle is *gone* for a week.

Out on a hunt, however, these rules are sorely tested. When a spruce chicken flaps noisily from the ground to a nearby tree branch, excitement can overwhelm training. That's why I don't mind them practicing so much.

Once, when I was chaperoning four young boys on one of their first hunts, a spruce hen gathering gravel for her crop didn't fly when the boys discovered her fifteen feet away. It was fall, vegetation was down, the shot was clear. They remembered to keep their barrels pointed away from each other. But their aim was trembling. They fired in a sustained fusillade. When the smoke had cleared the bird looked up and said, "Ba-bowk." (Spruce chickens are not noted for their smarts.) The boys fired again, and again, and again, shouting for bullets to reload. Finally the bird flew away.

We returned to practice on the shooting stump.

The way that we've finally discovered to recycle all that lead has been to dig it out with knives and hatchets and then to smelt it. At first we made decorative knives. The boys wanted suits of armor, but I convinced them that if they ever put on a lead breast plate they'd collapse to the ground with broken ribs.

What they do now is carve a form into a bole of birch—a star, a bird—and then pour into it the lead they've melted in a can over a bonfire. When they chisel away the wood the result is art.

There remains in the shooting stump enough lead to make a life-sized cast of a bear.

ΛΛΛ

This morning I saw icicles dripping in the sunlight. The snowcover was gone except for patches on north-facing ridge sides. Trees were greening. No rain had fallen for weeks. Icicles?

It had gotten below freezing during the night, obviously. But icicles don't bud in the spring like leaves.

I went closer. The icicles hung from the side of a leaning birch that had been gouged by another tree toppled during the winter past. The icicles were of birch sap, steadily welling.

I'd seen that sap oozing up out of stumps where I'd felled trees in the spring. It had always seemed like blood. But I'd never seen icicles of it. The color was of sun. When I went inside I carried one.

"This is made of birch syrup!" I said to the boys.

We all sucked on a piece. Sweet!

And then the boys went back to modifying the scopes on their rifles.

"I've never seen birch-sap icicles in all the years we've lived here," I said.

They looked up in deference to the eagerness in my tone. "Wow," they said, dutifully. They bent back to their work.

I wondered how I could help them understand the magic.

Magic is "the secret forces in nature" according to my elegant old Webster's.

Last month we found a moose newly dead a few yards from our trail to the road. It was an aged cow, her teeth worn and rotted. Ravens had begun gouging her eyes and tongue.

"Rad!" the boys decided after a moment's hesitation.

They checked all around the moose for predator tracks in the snow or a trail of blood atop it or some indication of how she had died. They tested the warmth of her hide to judge how long she'd been dead. They claimed rights to various body parts for the day when her skeleton would be picked clean. ("I want the hooves!" "I want the skull!" "No, *I* want the skull!")

Then they started back on the trail, talking about the snow cave they were building.

Again I wanted them to linger, to get the wonder of the moment.

A week or two after finding the moose we ran the dogs to the point where the trail crosses the creek to discover that the creek was wide open. The winter ice had melted away. All that remained was a ribbon of compacted snow the width of a dogsled suspended a foot and a half above the water. The hard-packed trail remained after the level of the creek fell.

We debated whether to try racing across it with the sled but decided to test its strength by sending a single dog first. We unclipped the lead dog from his trace and watched as he darted across the ice bridge.

The bridge crumbled away behind his rear paws as if in a cartoon. He made it to the other side, though, and didn't even look back.

"Man, is he cool!" the boys said in admiration of the dog's *sangfroid*.

I was more impressed by the fact that we had even considered crossing the ice bridge ourselves. The boys didn't seem to remember.

We walked across the cottonwood to the opposite shore,

then whistled for the rest of the team. The dogs plunged in and swam quickly to join us, pulling the sled behind them.

The next minute the boys were talking about remote-controlled cars.

It requires an effort for me to realize that the kids do, in fact, note the magic of their world, and honor it. I have judgments about what's more or less special. To them it's all of a piece, continuous, woven intimately together.

Trying to capture and hold one moment or another, trying to retain the uniqueness of one circumstance or another, is, in a way, tragic. That perspective assumes that some things matter more than others. Life becomes an addiction to Important Matters.

Adults ask questions like, "What was the best part?" "What did you like the most?" And the world gets divided up.

Originally and ultimately, I suspect, nothing isn't magic.

⋀⋀⋀

Recently I taught a course about *place* at Su Valley, home of the Rams, junior and secondary high school with a graduating senior class of, in total, with every senior graduating, twenty-two.

In Mrs. Porter's English class I asked what the kids thought of when they imagined this valley, their home.

"Where we live," was the initial reply. "Where our friends live."

Within a few minutes, however, I was writing on the blackboard responses like, "Where meaning becomes known, in social or physical setting." "What matters."

My project was to help the students make a video of what was important to them about the place they lived. Two girls immediately wanted to film the Homecoming basketball game. Another decided to film the mountains rising above the flood plain of the Susitna River. One boy tried to capture the sequence of a creek freezing to show the rapidity of change and the consequences of seasons.

Everyone liked the idea of getting up in a bush plane, panning across the wilderness of the valley, and then zooming in on the small clearing of the school.

The bus route to collect these kids covers more than a hundred road miles, winding down gravel roads, waiting at trailheads. They are the first generation of the original Caucasian settlers. Some of the kids live in fancy houses, some live in log cabins. Some have pro-development parents, some have environmentalist parents. Every one of Mrs. Porter's diverse students understood that how they saw their world would determine what their world was. And they didn't assume that what they valued would necessarily be what their parents did.

That was the best I could have asked. In the expanse of this upper valley there are only individuals. There is little consensus about anything.

But when the kids understand that looking closely at what exists is important, then there's hope—not for any particular political or economic desire, but for what there is.

COMMUNITY

The upper part of the Susitna Valley is four times the size of Hawaii's Oahu, twice the size of Rhode Island, bigger than Manhattan, Brooklyn, Queens, the Bronx, Staten Island, and Hoboken put together. Within that expanse are three small communities. One of those three communities isn't even on the map.

The current "Official State Map" put out by the Alaska Division of Tourism shows, instead, communities that no longer exist. "Petersville," once a mining camp, has been a ghost town for half a century, if a couple of old trailers and an abandoned air strip qualify as a "town." Along the Alaska Railroad tracks the former railroad construction camps of "Chulitna" and "Curry" are listed, though nothing's there.

Of the three communities, Talkeetna has the only post office with federal employees. Skwentna has a contract station inside a log cabin. Trapper Creek also has a contract station (not a substation, but a place rented by the U.S. Government for rural mail delivery and pick-up), but behind the counter within the little plywood building is a woman wearing a uniform of the U.S. Postal Service. She's a department store window mannequin, poised elegantly, wearing a trucker's cap. On the counter over which she watches while Mike, the owner of the contract, sorts mail, is an old teeter-totter scale for weighing letters, an open jar of "dried moose brains" (actually a large desiccated fungus, but it *looks* real), fresh goose eggs for sale, and a three-dollar bill with President Clinton's face on it.

Trapper Creek is a mile directly across the Susitna River from Talkeetna, but, lacking a bridge, the communities are as separate as if on opposing sides of a mountain range. The Anchorage-Fairbanks blacktop runs through Trapper Creek, which is why there are two gas/gifts'n'groceries stores on that road. Those two highway stops do most of their business in the summer tourist season. They are the "center" of the community.

Skwentna has even less of a downtown. It has no roads at all and is accessible only by boat or plane. Both Skwentna and Trapper Creek are less towns than geographic designations for hundreds of square miles of forest where not many people live. Trapper Creek stretches from the Susitna River to the Alaska Range. Skwentna encompasses the flatlands of the Yentna River, a major tributary of the Susitna.

Talkeetna is at the dead end of a fourteen-mile paved road that branches off the Anchorage-Fairbanks highway. It has a Main Street with three bars, four motels (two of them historic buildings), and five small restaurants. It has a volunteer fire department with a government-funded station full of equipment. It even has its own public radio station, mostly volunteer run, "serving the upper Susitna Valley since 1993." Its residents have an exceptionally strong sense of community, perhaps because of its town center, perhaps because it's where people in the more distant parts of the valley gravitate if they seek central community.

Most Trapper Creek and Skwentna residents pride themselves on being particularly independent. Yet even the most remote trapper or homesteader will have some identification with the nearest settlement.

All three communities will donate without reservation to residents of their general area who have had cabin fires or other catastrophes.

The real frontier, I've come to believe, is found not in the individual's interaction with wilderness, but in community.

"It is incumbent on those who retreat to the wilderness to heal in themselves the ills of the culture from which they've come," wrote Thomas Merton, who lived both in retreat and within the community of his Trappist order.

It is particularly incumbent on those who retreat to communities at the edge of wilderness to create what might have been lacking in the society they left. New land, last chance.

The upper valley is a center in Alaska of grassroots activism. Especially in Talkeetna, the motivation to organize is strong. There are environmental, pro-development, educational, and religious coalitions, each with clear ideas of what the area should become or remain.

In California's Big Sur, a handful of original settlers banded together fifty years ago to try to control both their own destiny and the land's. They succeeded. The ocean cliffs, grassy hills, and redwood canyons of that powerfully beautiful area have not been significantly altered by a constant stream of international tourism or currently astronomical real estate values. Vast open lands remain, as a result first of community consensus and now by law.

The communities of the upper Susitna Valley are the small frontier towns of America's earliest days: eager to establish themselves economically while trying to maintain the values they were founded on.

Those values remain from historic America: freedom, love of the land, trust in each other, and the very local need to create enough sources of income to survive.

Barter is not uncommon in the upper valley. Splitting firewood or peeling cabin logs are jobs more than a few residents first undertook upon arriving in the country. Some families lack any transportation—dog team, horse, or car—even though living along a road, which, in a rural area of scattered logistics, is indicative of deep poverty. But with oil revenue in Alaska accruing steadily, public school teachers can earn $50,000 a year, a local state trooper $70,000.

The unifying social factor is the lack of class distinction. There is no right or wrong side of the tracks in these communities, no high society. Everyone interacts as equals. A "land baron" out here is an old homesteader with four rusted pickups in front of a cabin on his 360 acres of hay, old-growth birch, and possibility.

The divisive factor within the communities is the argument for "a way my kids can make a living here, too." Since one man's economic struggle is another's chosen lifestyle close to the earth, since one man's traditional hunting ground is another's site for a new getaway recreational cabin, there is endless discussion about how to provide for everyone's needs.

Oddly, the endless debates keep the communities cohesive. In breakfast cafes, in the bars, at public meetings, people talk with each other, or talk at each other, but they communicate, or try to communicate, because the issues that affect these communities are critical, and immediate.

⋀⋀⋀

The meeting was held in the high-ceilinged, starkly-lit echo box of the Talkeetna Elementary School gym. Metal folding chairs were arranged in long rows from the center court line back to the concrete wall supporting a basketball backboard. The chairs faced three folding tables, set up end to end.

Representatives of the National Park Service and the State of Alaska sat at the tables, chatting among themselves. Ten minutes before the scheduled start of the meeting all the chairs were filled with locals in wool caps and down vests, unzipped parkas and minus-forty-degree Army surplus vapor-barrier boots. The gym was hot. Doors to the winter night were opened.

There had been many public meetings with various government agencies in the fifteen years since the road into town was paved. The meetings had discussed zoning ordinances and logging contracts and new roads, bridges, powerlines, and subdivisions. But not much had changed as a result. Some small tracts of land had been opened to homesteading or recreational cabin construction; almost all the land was still forest. A few timber stands had been allocated for firewood cutting or cabin-tree logging; no clear-cuts had ensued. Grand government plans for massive development—a domed city beneath the glaciers, a hydroelectric dam on the great Susitna River, moving the capitol of Alaska from Juneau to the lower valley—had not taken off, like dodo birds trying to fly.

Suddenly, however, the nature of the land and its communities was up for grabs, again.

At issue was a government proposal to build a complex of tourist developments across the upper valley: visitor centers, hotels, a ski resort, backcountry roads and trails and public use cabins. The plan was supported by Alaska's governor, all three Congressional delegates, the Susitna Valley borough, the National Park Service, and the multinational cruise-ship-bus-plane-and-train tour companies that package lucrative Alaskan vacations.

Some locals agreed; jobs would result. Most didn't; the land would be permanently altered, the town overwhelmed. Those who disagreed with the plan carried a revival-tent fervor into the gym. By the time the meeting began people were standing three deep against the walls.

First came "public testimony."

With a slight air of pugnacious defiance, with a clear but occasionally trembling voice, a dark-haired woman wearing backwoods clothes came up from the audience, sat at the table,

and spoke. "Little is known of the archaeology of this area because of the early demise of the Athabascan mountain people.
Around 1918 many, many people died from white people's disease: the measles, the whooping cough, the influenza. There
were three waves of sickness. And today we are also at risk to
suffer from white peoples' disease. It is greed. It is refusing to see
limits to the land until it is too late. Now our spirits are healthy.
We take strength from the trees, the animals, and the free open
spaces. What troubles me a lot about these proposed visitor
centers is what it would do to our spirit. Will we too suffer
from white men's disease?"

Spontaneously, the roomful of people applauded. Some of
the officials at the front tables visibly winced. They had come in
good faith to hear comments on the proposal. They'd been
hoping to avoid combat.

The next testimony was equally impassioned. The applause
was louder. Each speaker had prepared for his or her few minutes of testimony.

A man with the powerful build of a climber concluded his
speech with, "Aldo Leopold, widely recognized as the father of
wildlife management in this country, back in the '40s wrote,
'Recreational development is a job not of building roads into
lovely country, but of building receptivity into the still unlovely
human mind.' The people who are going to learn the most
about Denali, and who thus assure her of continued healthy existence, are not those who come here in droves as packaged accidental tourists, but who come with an acceptance of this
place, and a willingness to be a little humbled by it."

Foot stomping. Whistles.

A score more testimonies followed, all heartfelt, pleading
not to "turn this area into Yosemite or West Yellowstone," to
recognize that "the *spirit* of wilderness must be preserved."

A science teacher in the area high school ended his testimony by taking out his banjo and singing a song composed just
for the meeting. "C'mon, everyone, join me on the chorus!"

And the crowd did. "That National Park Service has got a lot of gall/ To try and turn our little town into a big strip mall."

Three times a speaker began by saying about the speaker immediately prior, "That's a tough act to follow."

An elementary school teacher performed a skit in which kids took part, lampooning what small-town life would be like if "mega-industrial tourism started pumping two thousand people a day through here."

Many speakers addressed the truth that in 1983 Denali National Park had been dramatically increased in size to include parts of the valley. Those "South Side" parklands had not been "opened up" as yet, which meant, everyone understood, roads and campgrounds and concession stands within the jurisdiction of the park, and the commensurate private developments of hotels, gift stores, gas stations, RV dumpsites, fast-food restaurants, and other such enterprise in the land surrounding the park.

One of the options the Park Service had initially considered was to leave the land wilderness. It would still be accessible by boat and foot and small plane and snowmachine and dogsled and ski and local guiding services, but not Winnebago, and not air-conditioned tour bus. The issue of "reasonable access" was at the heart of the debate.

"We're not anti-tourist," one local resident said. "The economy in the upper valley is based on tourism. Sixty-five million dollars a year comes into the area through small remote lodges and guiding services and fishing and outfitters. But the experience of Denali is not commensurate if seen through the window of a tour bus."

The voices that approved of the proposed developments anticipated local jobs. But of equal weight in the argument for development was, "How come the feds just lock up the land so no one can get at it?" Rural Alaska has traditionally been in opposition to almost any government except if direct benefits result.

But the overwhelming mood of the meeting was, "Let's keep what we've got. If we wanted large-scale development, we'd move back to where we came from. And the land is too important to trash."

A week later, Russ Berry, the head of Denali National Park, who had sat at the speaker's table through the entire meeting, called it, "A sad Ghost Dance for a world already lost."

The metaphor from the final stand of the Plains Indians against Manifest Destiny was apt. The upper Susitna Valley, facing the last wave of America's economic expansion across its own lands, has had only a small band of zealous "natives" to stand against what seems inevitable: more of what's everywhere in the wilderness valley, too.

But this world, rather than "already lost," has only recently been found.

The result of that meeting and other grassroots efforts was unexpected: the government proposals went back to the drawing board. The scale of development to dramatically increase tourism in the Susitna Valley region of Denali National Park was reduced. A motley assortment of guides and trappers and fishermen and homesteaders and school teachers and log-cabin builders won the battle.

It was, however, only one battle in a bigger war. After two years of quiescence, serious new proposals have been advanced to build big. Again.

There will be more meetings.

Where are the reinforcements?

ᴧᴧᴧ

Ten miles north of Talkeetna is an area known as Chase. Seventy-five years ago it was a railroad construction camp, like Chulitna and Curry. Now it is one of the parts of the valley where a few families live "semi-subsistence." That means they get the basis of their food from the land—hunting, fishing, berry picking, gardening—while working seasonal jobs elsewhere for limited cash needs.

Those twenty or thirty people live widely scattered, usually in cabins they built themselves. They chose the area across the Talkeetna River from the village because only the railroad bridge spans the river. There are no roads to the area. There never have been.

As in other remote parts of the valley, some land has been sold by the state or borough to satisfy Alaskan residents' demand for ownership, mainly for recreational property. The parcels sold have ranged from five acres to forty. All the people living around Chase acquired their land between 1968 and 1984 when such lands, after statehood, became available. Hundreds of other parcels in the area are owned by people living elsewhere, many now not even in the state. Those tracts are indistinguishable from the rest of the forest, except for the aluminum survey pipes driven into the ground that mark the property lines.

Over the last five years most of the actual residents of the area compiled a "Chase Comprehensive Plan," a hundred-page document detailing their desires for the region where they live. Some of the conclusions are, "Manage natural resources in support of a local subsistence economy." "All use of the area should respect and be compatible with the natural environment." "All existing lifestyles and land use patterns will be preserved."

One critical method to accomplish those desires is this: "Since an important element of the Overall Goal of the Plan is to discourage roads into the area, physical surface access requirements will be satisfied by trails."

The valley's borough and the state would like to build roads across the Talkeetna River. Property values would increase. Absentee owners, far in the majority, would benefit.

Here, then, is a classic Alaskan lifestyle conflict.

It's also the classic American conflict, but now that the original Indian Nations in the Lower Forty-eight have been corralled into reservations, the only remaining venue of all the United States is Alaska.

Is it possible to choose and to live a non-industrial, roadless, independent life free of supermarkets, gas stations, and power lines? Yes.

Is it common? Hardly.

But is it worthy, with all the rest of the world in pursuit of quick economic development? That is yet to be decided.

Thomas Berry, a Catholic environmental theologian and author of the influential book *The Dream of the Earth,* suggests that "the dynamism of our consumer society is the supreme pathology of all of history."

"Use of the term 'supreme pathology,'" he continues, "can be justified by the observation that the (environmental and industrial) change that is taking place in the present is not simply another historical transition or another cultural transformation. Its order of magnitude is immensely more significant in its nature and in its consequences. We are indeed closing down the major life systems on the planet. We are acting on a geologic and biological order of magnitude. We are changing the chemistry of the planet . . . . Ever-heightened consumption [is seen as] the way to ultimate human fulfillment."

To begin counterbalancing this human propensity toward an always greater gross national product, to begin returning some equilibrium to an overmined, overlogged, and overrun planetary system, the politics of wilderness was introduced in the early part of this century.

But you can't make a home in a national park.

And so some people in this valley made sustainable homes on lands they see less as "state" or "national" or "borough" or "private" than nurturing. If any human ownership can be claimed, the land belongs to the mountain Athabascans, the first and only people to have lived near Chase until the Alaska Railroad was built. But they're all dead. They lived a subsistence lifestyle for hundreds of years, until the railroad.

The current residents use kerosene and steel in addition to caribou and moose. But the heart's the same. The values are the same. The respect for the land and all its inhabitants is the same.

As far as much of Native America is concerned, the entire environmental movement is just white people finally beginning to put down roots on this continent.

Instead of extracting wealth and moving on, the truth that there's nowhere else to go is sinking in, slowly. The people north of Talkeetna who organized their Comprehensive Plan have their backs against a wall. If their document is indication, they certainly have the acumen and resources to be successful corporate lawyers. But they choose instead to dry salmon and pick berries.

May their tribe increase.

∧∧

Talkeetna, pop. 490, wants to try an experiment.

The administrators and teachers of the elementary school unanimously want to become as sophisticated and educationally innovative as an expensive private school. At no charge.

They want to downplay competition among their students in favor of cooperation, mutual support, and the hope of having each student work toward personal fulfillment rather than have that success be based on the failure of others.

They want to get grade designations in favor of having each kid work at his or her own level. They want their students to end up happy and whole rather than driven and compulsive.

I don't remember any of these ideas as being part of my public grade school. I had Mrs. Janowitz, who arranged our seats each Monday morning based on who did best on Friday's spelling test. The smart ones sat in front. Dumb in back. Others' failure was my fulfillment. I felt superior when I won and vengeful when I lost. I *cared* about grades.

And I hated school.

If my parents had had enough money they could have sent me to a fancy private school where individual nurture can be bought.

For a rural public school to shift the paradigm of learning

from bell-curve competition to cooperative effort is appropriate for the social context. A rural village, to maintain its existence, requires cooperative effort, requires the practice of cooperation, of consensus, or fragmentation grows. It grows into a big sprawling town, which is what most people left in favor of a remote little village.

But there's opposition to the curriculum from outside the school.

Some residents of Talkeetna see the approach as *different*. It isn't what parents grew up with. Difference can be threatening.

Talkeetna has people who climb extreme routes in the Alaska Range and people who think climbing is crazy. Talkeetna has business people who want more business and people who love their isolation. Talkeetna has beer drinkers and religious zealots, tremendous community love and wild community antagonism.

And in the middle are the children.

"What we are trying to do," says Erin Aulman, the school's principal, "is give our kids the skills they need to be successful anywhere. The corporate world in America now values cooperation, like village life. A manager needs to know how to get along with his or her workers. Executive seminars try to teach understanding, not dominance."

I grew up trying to dominate. I won. I went to Harvard on full scholarship and got an executive-level job in New York City. When I realized how much I had lost by winning, I moved to the north woods. I'm still trying to learn the skills of understanding and unity.

If I had been helped in grade school to learn kind communication instead of just long division and the names of the Presidents...well, goodness, what a staggering thought. I'd have been a better parent from the beginning. I'd have found my confidence and happiness in who I was rather than what I achieved. Much would be radically different.

The Talkeetna grade school's experiment doesn't seem to

be fraught with much risk. But it is predicated on great faith. Even if it doesn't ultimately work, the kids have already been spared teachers like Mrs. Janowitz, and have been shown that they can be valued just for who they are.

ΛΛΛ

It's the season for the buses to begin stopping at the Trapper Creek Trading Post again.

The buses carry tourists. The tourists need rest stops. The Trading Post, like the half-dozen other cafe/gas'n'grocery stores on the road between Anchorage and Denali Park, gets its share of buses. Forty to fifty people per bus, all new to Alaska, all carrying vouchers stamped by their industrial tour company for scheduled hotels, meals, and transportation. They're glad to investigate a little bit of "real" Alaskan life.

When you've come all the way to Alaska by plane or cruise ship and then take a tour of the state from, by, in, and around a bus, the Trading Post is one of those places that can help make a vacation.

It has old log cabins in the woods behind the store. Wildflowers line the driveway and fuschias hang from the porch. Its one vintage gas pump is protected from the elements by a sagging, gray wood overhang that has seen a lot of weather. There is even a collapsed barn where the school district used to park its school buses until the roof fell in last year under heavy snows. Now there is just twisted metal and split wood and five dented yellow school buses.

It makes a good snapshot. "And this picture here's a whole big barn that just fell right down because they get so much snow up there in Alaska. Isn't that something?"

There are bigger places where the tour buses stop on the road, places with large dining rooms and satellite-dish television and lots of dead animals hung on the walls or flanking the doors. Tourists are supposed to like dead stuffed animals.

But because the Trading Post is so far from Anchorage it

remains homey and a little slow. The tourists like that ambience, and relax.

Judy and Buddy, the owners, are kind and friendly. They still *tahlk lahk thur in Tinnassee,* but they've been in Alaska fifteen years. They've given everyone in Trapper Creek credit at their store. Well, almost everyone. Locals will walk into the store, take a candy bar or muffin, sit down with some coffee, and finally, just before leaving, stop by the cash register to recall what they've had. It's like stopping by a neighbor's house to raid the fridge.

This has been the first year that a hand-lettered sign went up behind the counter: "Charges must be Paid by the tenth of the Month. Judy." Until the buses start coming, money is tight.

Tourism is the basis of the economy in the upper valley. Skwentna and Talkeetna have the majority of the hunting and fishing lodges, the guides and outfitters, the air taxi services. Trapper Creek has buses in the summer. Like the Queen Elizabeth docking at a lazy Third World port, the highway liners slip between the locals' little rust buckets that have cracked windshields and chipped paint. The regulars inside the Trading Post quickly get another cup of coffee before the passengers disembark.

Most of the visitors head straight to the washrooms. Judy and Buddy have just added two more. The original two have showers in them, for locals without running water. Two dollars per shower. Three dollars for shower and towel. The other passengers line up for coffee or take the side door into the liquor store to buy a single-shot bottle or two. It's a long ride from Anchorage to Denali Park.

Almost everyone is elderly and almost everyone's experience of Alaska has been limited to color brochures, "postcard videos," tour guide interpretations, and The Real Alaska Salmon Bake wedged between tall buildings in downtown Anchorage.

The tourists often seem giddy when they stumble off the bus. They are talkative.

"Isn't this *just* like that TV show about Alaska?"

"Look! They have moose nugget earrings!"

"And what do you *do* here all winter?" a blue-haired grandma asks a grizzled local.

"Well not a whole lot," he says, scratching his chin.

"How *wonderful!*" she exclaims.

∿∿

"Oh God no. Don't write about that," said a distant neighbor.

"Better be real careful," said another. "People will get mad if you talk about it."

People are already mad. Nuts, too.

A dark secret in Trapper Creek has divided the community. It isn't alcohol or child abuse. It's . . . a library.

Trapper Creek voted against a publicly funded library some ten years ago. The vote was fifty-one to fifty. There were threats against those who wanted one. There was rage and resentment on both sides. Feuds were born, and remain.

Recently the issue came up again. There's an opportunity to accept a government grant to stock a library. And even those who want to take it are hesitant. Wrath is hard to endure.

Trapper Creek has a population of about 250. No one really knows the count because some people live too far back in the woods for census takers. Trapper Creek encompasses maybe 600 square miles. No one in the area seems to know exactly what the boundaries are. "Between the river and the mountains," is accurate enough.

People who live in Trapper Creek have decided to get away from the hubbub of urban life. For that matter, they've decided to get away from the hubbub of village life, too. Old Talkeetna, a mile across the river but thirty miles by road, is both a bustling tourist attraction and the center for all Denali climbs.

People who live in Trapper Creek are usually quite competent at the lives they've chosen. A few homesteaders with road access work their land for commercial potatoes or hay. There are professional trappers and log builders and mushers.

It's this self-reliance that is at the heart of the library controversy.

Building a library requires government money. People came to Trapper Creek to get away from government. Needless to say, Trapper Creek is "unincorporated." There is no town hall or mayor.

So a library built with government funds is viewed with suspicion. It's a way for Big Government to get its foot in the door. But what's worse is what might come after a library should it be built. Let me whisper: *taxes.*

How else would a small community keep a library running?

A self-reliant person who's come to the geographic frontier to carve out his own niche is loathe to accept handouts. But the idea of paying for other people is next to death. Even if it's just a few dollars a year, it's the principle of the thing. And it's by our principles that most of us live here.

It remains absurd to me that anyone would righteously send back a check for $75,000 earmarked for a library and books when everyone eagerly accepts the $700 to $1000 check in Permanent Fund oil revenue disbursement that the state hands out each year to every Alaskan.

I'm afraid it's inevitable that Trapper Creek stock a library with encyclopedias and magazines and novels that teach about the rest of the world. It's inevitable because human curiosity and reason are as compelling as the hunger for independence.

Give me liberty and give me books.

ΛΛΛ

Wasilla, 99654, pop. 4,400, has voted to levy its first-ever sales tax. The 2% tax will fund a police department.

Wasilla looks like a much bigger community than 4,400. It services contiguous suburban (to Anchorage) communities of similar populations. It has almost all the valley's commerce, including three different large supermarket strip malls.

One of those malls had a bank of four pay phones inside. Teenagers had been occasionally messing with them. Petty vandalism. The phones were removed. That was one of the specific reasons Wasilla voted itself a police force: to manage such crimes.

Wasilla doesn't have street gangs or drug wars. It's like a sprawling suburb of newly built subdivisions. The median age is about twenty-five: earnest young families working hard to achieve the American dream of a nice house, two cars, and multi-channel television.

So what happens when crime begins to get a little out of hand in such a town? Does the community become more unified? Does neighbor watch after neighbor? Do friends keep an eye on each other's property and do parents keep an eye on each other's children?

Yes, when values are clear.

Wasilla, however, voted to entrust those values to appointed authorities.

Since the vote was almost a dead heat, there are certainly many residents who refused to ask hired help do their work for them.

But as Wasilla has boomed, other priorities have superceded the original ones. People are honestly busy. Besides, "progress can't be stopped." A pleasant checkout woman at the supermarket offered that explanation to me when I asked her what she thought of the vote.

Of course "progress" can be stopped. War and resentment and another new mall can be stopped, too, if we so choose. They're all choices. They don't just happen.

Wasilla not long ago was a small town where few people locked their doors. Now it's a bigger town with police to create security instead of relying on neighborly trust. It will become a city if the growth continues. That progression is hardly unusual.

But to watch it happening just down the road, as it were, to watch the trees fall and backhoes dig septic pits and street lights sprout along old trails, and to see it happening so quickly it's as if in time-lapse photography (a few years ago Wasilla had no traffic lights; now it has five)...it feels already as if no one is really in control, just coping.

/\\/\\/\\

"Aw, hey man. I didn't know it was closed to Kings here."

That's the most popular excuse for taking salmon illegally. It comes in three different tones of voice: innocent and whiningly hurt at being accused; offended and blusteringly righteous about how hard it is to understand the regulation book; or aggressive and borderline violent, *maaaad* at being caught red-handed and ready to fight.

The next most popular excuse is a belch, followed by throwing a beer can.

But the worst excuse, the one that makes me smolder, is also the friendliest, the least mendacious. "I *live* around here. I'm a local!"

The upper valley is where salmon finally spawn after a journey of thousands of miles from the ocean past seine nets and set nets and commercial guides and weekend sport fishermen in the lower river system.

I've watched some of my neighbors study a run of Kings into their spawning grounds, calculate as best they can the ratio of males to females and the size of the run, and then, if the population is strong, zip out a bullet snagging hook to take one. That kind of fishing is based on the premise that the majority of fish must be allowed to breed. It's illegal, but a clear morality is operating. A sense of honor toward the resource is evident. The alternative is to travel fifty miles away to catch the same fish before it gets closer to home.

When I've seen that, I've turned my back.

What snaps me into vigilante anger is when I see lowlifes ripping fish after fish from shallow pools. They do it because they don't understand and they don't care. They think they can get away with it. They fill coolers that then fill their freezers or smokers.

The stock gets depleted. The fish stop coming back in the same numbers. Some years the fish don't come back at all.

There is ample evidence that even prehistoric times were chock-full of brainless morons. The woolly mammoth and the Alaskan musk ox were hunted to extinction. Certainly in historic times we're witnessing the devastation of many other species at our own hands.

The argument that "I live here" is specious. It's easy to feel proprietary toward a local creek or fishing hole. But a subsistence lifestyle does not warrant destruction of one's "own" resources. And when everyone's local hole is fished out, the finger of blame will be pointed all around.

Living in community is a way to sustain both everyone within it and everything around it. When community is functional, it satisfies a planetary need for consensus, compassion, and foresight.

NEIGHBORS

There are many unusual people in this remote valley. That's as tactfully as I can say it.

There are survivalists with cabins stocked like National Guard armories. There are adventurers who concoct expeditionary "firsts" to then pitch their exploits to *National Geographic.* There are enterprising businessmen hoping for a boom in riverboat tourism or bush plane flight-seeing. There are loonies and whackos from God-knows-where who were given one-way tickets out of their original towns, young and vivacious school teachers eager to Make A Difference in a rural area, retired laborers who drink themselves into a stupor every evening, commercial salmon fishermen, hunting guides, ivory carvers and a jazz composer.

The common trait among them all is this: everyone's different. Very different.

There have been gunfights to the death to resolve personal feuds. There are often friendly softball tournaments. Fundamentalist Christians and long-haired dopers go fishing together.

Living at the edge of conventional society makes it easy to be a character, and to be accepted. There aren't many of us out here. "Eccentric" is not an oft-used word. There is no value judgment in the term "neighbor." It's used often.

∧∧∧

"This has got to be the most beautiful spot for a home in the world," I said, standing in the front yard.

From the bluff above the Susitna River the autumnal forest rose beyond the water to white mountains.

"Without a doubt," said Arthur. He's lived, if only briefly, on Denali's South Buttress, overlooking a sizable part of Alaska.

"I agree," said my wife Lucia. She's lived in the liana highlands of Central America, bordered by blue oceans.

When celebrities have visited Talkeetna they've been brought to this house site, for effect. When local weddings have been in need of that perfect place to exchange vows, they've used the front yard.

But the price for that small promontory overlooking paradise has been high.

The river has been inexorably eating away the bluff. Only a fraction of the original acreage remains. Twice in ten years the cabin has had to be moved away from the edge of the crumbling river embankment. Then this summer, when the river had gnawed to within three yards of the house, the house burned to the ground. The cause remains a mystery. Nothing within was saved.

As they say in Bangladesh, when it rains it pours.

Talkeetna responded generously with donations for new building materials and volunteer help to get things underway. We were some of the volunteers out to admire the view and notch a few joists.

By the end of the day I'd come to admire, much more than the view, the woman who owned the land.

When her first son was an infant and the second still in the womb the boys' father died on the way down from the summit of Everest. The boys, now ten and eight, are bright and competent, but, as single mothers say, a *handful*. In addition to trying to raise them right, make a living, and shore up the riverbank each year with sandbags and cabled trees, Kathy's had to manage the formidable stress of doing it all by herself, as a single woman in a remote village.

Talkeetna's three home-based video rental businesses (television reception is poor-to-impossible) carry the same movies, so when a stormbound January comes with nothing to watch at night, people gossip. Kathy's attractive: tall, lean, and blue-eyed. She's not a recluse, which opens her to scrutiny from people who have nothing else to do.

Small town life can be nurturing and supportive, but it's also an occasional sinkhole of petty jealousies, resentments, and biases.

Single women out here usually pair up with men quickly, or leave. To remain single for a decade and hold a family together is extremely unusual in this area. It's also, obviously, exhausting.

The loss of the house and everything in it, with no insurance coverage, could well have been the last strand in a frayed cord snapping. It wasn't. Instead of the kids going to stay with relatives in the Lower Forty-eight while beleaguered Mom went into terminal shock, they all made a camp of tents and tarps beside the river and got down to work on the new place.

What seemed even more amazing is that now, still, with the nonstop grind of peeling logs and sanding corners and tar-sealing cement blocks, there remained in her during that time an acceptance of things-as-they-are that borders on grace.

While the boys helped peel bark but mostly played atop the long stack of spruce logs, I watched their mom hold a chainsaw over her head to trim some high log ends. Sawdust and clots of chain-saw oil spattered against her. And she was singing.

That's when I started to think that the most beautiful

horizons weren't those evident across the river plain but rather those in a woman's heart that allowed her to sing when just waking up in the morning should have been a struggle.

"Look how much peeling I've done!" cried one of the boys.

"Gonna be a bright, bright sunshiny day," sang their mom.

She's been a ski instructor, a mountain climber, a riverbank laborer, and now a house builder. Like many women who live in bush Alaska, she is *strong*. Her greatest strength, however, is in trying to find the stamina to sustain both home and family independent of convention.

ʌʌʌ

Some of the local kids think that Vince, with his white hair and long white beard, is Santa Claus.

Certainly no one is kinder than Vince. And it's true that at Christmas Vince wears a red velvet suit and thrills kids with presents that local businesses give him to distribute.

But Santa himself hides out most of the year and so has no good stories to tell.

Vince is always doing something new, and has a million stories. He is not shy about telling them. To anyone. At any time. For the slightest reason.

When he was younger Vince roamed Alaska as a surveyor (Have Transit, Will Travel) mainly to roam the state. It was his way to see Umiat on the North Slope, and Yentna Station in the valley when there was still a little gold-mining activity there. When he retired to Trapper Creek he still did some survey work because it allowed him to race a tractor-treaded off-road vehicle across a flooded creek when only a pan of ice separated him from death.

That story involves one of his sons and a four-year-old granddaughter. The three of them were out in the upper valley on a late winter job when they returned to a creek that had begun breaking up. There was enough ice left for his son and granddaughter to cross. Vince sent them over with a sleeping bag with which to await rescue. He thought he might have a chance to drive the machine across, but if he broke through, they'd survive. It would make a great story to go out on.

He made it across.

He's seventy-five now, and tells that story with the glee and excitement of a kid. He was seventy-two when it happened.

It seems to be an unspoken code among outdoorsmen here (and more than a few haven't a clue what's beyond their home, bar, and truck cab) to acquire adventurous stories that then get polished across the years. After a certain age, those with tales becomes raconteurs. Some take more prodding, some less, to "tell the one about...." Vince takes no prodding.

These days Vince contents himself with building...something. It's three stories tall, four wings wide, and modelled after a carnival Fun House. There are unfinished rooms everywhere. Vince isn't ready to retire to television and cats. He's "keeping busy by pounding nails." He's outside every day for most of the day.

Recently my twelve-year-old and I heard the *whump* of a snow load fall from part of his roof as we passed. I said, "That's either Vince's roof sliding or Vince."

My son said, matter-of-factly, "Vince wouldn't fall."

"Good morning!" calls Vince from the peak of the roof, waving a shovel. "How'dya like that avalanche? Pretty neat, huh?"

At seventy-five he still clambers around thirty feet off the ground wearing a red stocking cap, "keeping busy."

I never know what I'm going to find him up to. Well, almost never. What I'm sure about is that he is constantly looking for a way to help *anyone*. He's the model for the friendly, helpful, Alaskan old-timer.

A broken-down car on the highway with a family inside lacking money for repairs? A gold mine! Vince scoops them up, drives them a hundred miles to Wasilla, buys the parts they need, and drives them back. He tells stories the whole way, stories about the land and his experience of it.

Weekenders from the city uncertain about which way to start a hike? Follow Vince! There's a moose kill just a mile back that a griz has been feeding off, definitely a good place to investigate from a distance. And if the bear happens to still be around, it'll make a good story later.

Offering help is not a duty, but a joy.

He's quick to reveal, though, that there are some things for which he has no compassion. The IRS seems to come up frequently in his conversation when he's needing an epithet for emphasis. Government bureaucracies in general are topics for loud discourse.

But that's not an unusual perspective in rural Alaska.

What's unusual anywhere is the sort of honest kindness that seems like an offered gift.

The standard clichés of the abrupt urbanite, the laconic cowboy, and the friendly rural Alaskan have bases in truth. But Vince is the closest I've found here to someone so happy at being amidst the land that his garrulous generosity is a natural extension of that love.

/W\

Louis XIV builds Versailles. He makes it *big*. That way he figures it'll be impressive. He wants people to say, "Hey, wow, I'm impressed."

Mad King Ludwig with his fairy-tale-towered Bavarian castle, William Randolph Hearst with his palatial estate called San Simeon—same thing.

Compared to what Orv has done, they're all preposterously exaggerated. Orv doesn't build for effect. The places he has created were built for their own sake, built mostly by himself. And they're as impressive as any grand poobah's palace.

The homestead he's now finished in a roadless part of the valley came after he built a retreat on a tiny island just off the southern Alaska coast.

The grounds of the five-acre island he owns are as beautifully and minimally landscaped as a Japanese moss garden, matted with berry bushes and wildflowers. The oldest of the four structures amidst it was constructed from an old beached barge's massive timbers, laboriously pried loose and floated on tides to the island. The newest building is powered by a small hydroelectric plant fueled by a gravity-fed water line falling 500 feet from a mountain cascade on the mainland.

In none of the construction is there evidence of construction. The roots of huge spruce entwine with and conceal rebar-reinforced concrete pilings. The steps ten yards up from the rock beach aren't hewn. They're natural footholds in tidal-washed stone.

And yet there's a solar power system in addition to the hydro. There are hot showers and a food cooler chilled with water circulated from the hydro line. There's even an honest-to-goodness flush toilet that empties into the sea.

The architecture and engineering and plumbing and carpentry and electrical wiring and general labor were without subcontractor. A writer for *Sunset* magazine, investigating rumors, once leaped onto the rock beach to beg for a feature story. Orv's response was modest but firm, and backed by a rifle. Retreats are not showcases.

To get building materials to the homestead site in the valley, Orv had to fly. He's an accomplished pilot in addition to a competent mariner. He even flew his dogteam to the site, a few dogs at a time, until trails could be established.

Again he built "small," but nothing is lacking. The elegance of the place is the way it, too, fits into its environment. It is the only homestead I've ever seen in Alaska that does *not* have junk strewn in the yard.

Orv built it after retirement. He had taught public school, not been CEO of a major construction company.

This is a guy who has done and continues to do just about everything one can in Alaska, from raising children to raising oysters, mushing in the high Arctic to mining in the mountains. And he's done it well.

The Seven Wonders of the World required thousands of workers. Men built *big* as monuments to themselves. The pyramids will last longer than an isolated cabin built of old barge timber or a homestead on a lake in the woods. But the legacy of one man's individual accomplishment has greater resonance for me.

Craft is for the sake of the crafting, not a magazine spread. A full life is lived, not designed. The deepest impression is made by not trying to impress.

∿∿

"John McCafferty," he said, extending a hand as he got in the passenger side of the car. His grip was bony but firm. He was clean-shaven, maybe sixty, with the taut, translucent skin of serious alcoholics. He carried a blanket wadded into a ball that he'd been hugging with both arms. He looked me in the eye as he said his name, and his gaze was clear. "Thanks for picking me up."

I shook hands and said, "I'm Rick and this is Forrest, who is almost three and almost asleep." I gestured to the back seat.

"No, I'm *eleben*," said Forrest, holding up four fingers without opening his eyes.

"Sorry," I said. "Eleven-year-olds don't take naps. Except today."

The man turned around in his seat and studied the child drifting back to sleep. I pulled back onto the highway.

"That's what I both regret for myself and validate as my only consistent wisdom," he said after a long minute. "I would have loved to have had children, but I haven't been able to maintain a coherent emotional stability."

I found myself staring at him. Whoa! Where does a hitch-hiking street person acquire that kind of language?

In answer to my implicit curiosity, he said, casually, as if rendering the plot of a book or reciting a familiar speech, "John McCafferty, only child of a North Carolina traveling salesman, a suicide when I was six. Nervous breakdown in Korea, too much death, too hard to make sense of it, alcoholic for twenty years, drifting around, sad, in and out of institutions, then I found God and I've been sober ever since but still a little off, not a lot, just enough, like carrying this blanket against the chill." He grinned. "I've got my Metamucil and a change of clothes wrapped up in here."

"Where are you headed?"

He pointed vaguely ahead. "Out of town. Into the hills. Shelter keeps me warm but it doesn't feed the soul, if you know what I mean. Did you know that John Muir carried only bread and a blanket when he went into the hills? Scotsman, too. We travel light. The baggage is in our hearts. Are you a Christian?"

I was caught off guard. "Well, sure."

"Then let me say a prayer."

He bowed his head and spoke clearly. "Dear Lord, let me stay aware of my limitations so I don't climb too high and pull others down with me when I fall. Let me stay free of the booze that makes me crazier. Let me find peace in just who I am. Amen."

I nearly laughed aloud, not in mockery or judgment, but from unexpected pleasure. I'd never before heard anyone offer a prayer for himself to a stranger. I had expected the usual, "Dear Lord, bless this guy who gave me a ride and help him give me five bucks." I liked the idea of staying aware of small blessings instead of seeking greater merit.

"Yeah," he continued. "I count it as wisdom to keep remembering that I don't have all the resources to be a good father. We don't need any more occasionally good fathers, or mothers. I certainly am not content with all that I am, but I've tried all the anti-psychotics and they make me suicidal. I do the best I can with what I've been given, even if most people don't count that as much."

I started to say something supportive, like, "You seem a good man to me," but he kept up his patter.

"Consistently good, the continuity of goodness—that's what I don't see much of anywhere. I might just be projecting my own variability, but if what matters doesn't have continuance, then we need God's succor, or to step in retreat to the hills."

We rode in silence for a while. At first I thought about his words. Then I tried to imagine how to respond, to say something kind. It finally occurred to me that he didn't particularly need my help, except for a lift.

"One step, twelve steps, whatever," he suddenly said. "As long as we see the ground we're walking on. You can let me out here if you don't mind."

I slowed the car.

"Thanks for listening," he said. "Thanks for not offering advice. God bless us all."

When I stopped he opened the door, tugged on the pants slipping down on his narrow hips, readjusted his wadded blanket, and started walking up the greening hills.

ᴧᴧᴧ

A few hours ago I was nearly shot by a razor-tipped arrow. And I was glad, in time. But not at first.

I had decided to take advantage of a break in the rain to hike the three miles to the house of our only neighbors. They have been out of the state for many years, but the house still needs checking twice a year—once in summer against bears, and once in winter to shovel the snow from the roof. They're friends, so I'm glad to make sure their place is secure.

I walked down the ridge from our home, forded the creek that was getting low again after a week of rain, pushed through tall grasses, and angled up over the opposite ridge toward their house. There wasn't a trail, but there were lots of high bush cranberries, which I ate as I went.

When I got near the crest of the hill where they had built their house, I stumbled out of the brush onto their wide trail. Though it was somewhat grown over, it was still easy walking. I'd been calling "Yo!" along the creek to alert bears to my passage, but I stopped on the way up their hill for no special reason. It's balm at times to walk quietly and listen.

Then I came around an alder-thicket bend and saw an arrow pointed at my heart.

Immediately, the guy holding the bow turned his aim aside and released the tension from the draw. But "immediately," when an arrow is aimed at your chest, seems to take a few hours.

"Whoa!" I said, involuntarily, more an exhalation than a communication.

"Sorry," said the guy, getting up from where he'd been kneeling. "It's all right."

I tried to straighten my wobbly legs.

He was in his thirties, dressed in camouflage, with a camouflage hat and camouflage bow. He had a number of days' growth of beard.

I carry a prejudiced view of most hunters who come to this valley for moose or bear. As often as not "hunters" on all-terrain vehicles motor up and down tundra waiting for an animal to appear in the distance. Then they run it down and blast it. Or blast it and then run it down. A moose quarter atop an ATV will sink the tires into tundra deeply enough to leave permanent grooves. Tundra is fragile and regenerates slowly. But it's still legal to run these machines virtually anywhere. That's incomprehensible.

A lot of hunting simply would not happen without the small but powerful vehicles. Pilots will even put them inside float planes, land on remote lakes, and then the posse will putt off after big game. Real hunting, of course, has absolutely nothing whatsoever to do with machines.

"Bull tracks," said the guy, gesturing down. "Today's. He's

close. Firm front track. He's carrying a big one." His tone was apologetic, explaining himself.

He meant that the moose had a big rack.

I am outraged by motor-vehicle hunting, but just perplexed by trophy hunting. A "world record" moose rack is often more important than the animal's meat. This is plainly such a perversion of the original intent of the hunt that it's too sick to address directly. "So, little dick, huh?" seems pointless to say.

The camouflaged guy and I had some serious talking to do.

"How'd you get back here?" I said, standing taller.

He waved a hand. "Been stalking for two days. This bull's been covering a lot of ground."

"You drive up this trail?" I asked. I was protecting my neighbor's route to the road.

He smiled. "I don't hunt like that," he said. "This trail hasn't been used in at least three years. Except by game." Then he asked, "And do you always hunt with Counter Assault?"

That was the brand of pepper spray I carried.

"I live here," I said.

He nodded. "I can tell by the way you were walking. But you don't live up there," indicating the top of the hill where the unused trail led.

I began to relax my defenses. This guy had something going on that wasn't common.

"By the way I was walking?"

"Confident. Familiar. Not afraid."

"OK," I said. "You're not a complete jackass."

He laughed aloud. "Really, I'm sorry I had the bow drawn. I'm embarrassed. I knew you weren't the moose, but I had no idea anyone was out here. I haven't seen any sign. Can I offer you some tea?" He turned around and picked up a thermos.

For a half-hour we sat talking.

He had been raised in western Montana and had arrived in Alaska a few years ago. He worked construction in Anchorage but spent his weekends in the woods. He'd twice been to wilderness "schools" to study tracking, and hunted alone, without a gun or off-road vehicle. He left antlers in the woods. He didn't even like the idea of selling them to make tourist curios. He hadn't eaten store-bought meat in fifteen years.

Although neither he nor I said it, we would have agreed that hunting is communion. It's not a game and not a battle and hardly a sport. The communion contains elements that are, in fact, holy: a union with the natural world and with the life that supports life, the animal that offers its flesh for sustenance.

The last time I had accidentally met someone anywhere near our home was ten years prior in winter when a bozo on a snowmachine drove up to the house babbling helplessly. He had been "lost" in the woods and hadn't the brains to head in one direction, until he came upon our dogsled trail and followed it to "rescue."

The hunter with his bow reminded me that there remain people who go into the woods not for "sport" or to "recreate," but to experience the mysteries of the world fully.

THE NECESSARY AND SENTIENT SLED DOG

And now an alternative perspective, an op-ed view, a word from another realm: woof.

Every different civilization, culture, race, and social history offers insight into the mysteries of the world.

But when have you ever read a history of the world from the point of view of dogs? Or bears (who have been *really* shafted from time immemorial, and continue to get shot on sight or "relocated" without any voice in the matter)? Or trees? Do trees have rights? Damned right they do. Or should. Not often, though, in an anthropocentric universe.

Imagine the Alaska Congressional delegation not clamoring to cut forests for human gain, but opening a discussion to consider what individual trees might desire for their lives. Goofy, huh? It might not be that farfetched, though, in time.

The evolution of human moral consciousness has been gradually to accept the legitimate rights first of other groups of people (serfs and slaves, "foreigners," women, children), then individual people (Federal Government vs. Bob), next to admit large mammals such as whales and caribou into the clique of Beings (as opposed to Things), and just recently to debate the status of precious ecosystems (coral reefs, coastal plains, redwood groves).

This is a clear continuum, moving from a completely insular "me and only me" perspective to an identification with other species and systems of life.

John Muir climbed a redwood during a wild storm to sway from the upper branches just to see what it was like, to be a tree. I've not acquired that piney perspective, though it does sound intriguing. For me the spruce and birch and alder that surround the house are often simply *there*, like the mountains: subliminally reassuring.

Dogs are my touchstone for consistent entry to the non-human world. Often I think of what they think as they lie in their houses under trees around the house. They can stare at the woods for an entire rainy day, ears periodically twitching off mosquitoes, noses glassing the terrain, as it were, for subtle changes. When I go out to feed them or play with them or check to see what they've leaped up to bark furiously toward (a scent or sound invisible in the forest) I know that their perceptions are fantastically different from mine. And it's frustrating only being able to project what those perceptions might be. Anthropomorphizing the world is a limited source of insight.

These dogs are as close to wild as pet dogs get. They're the size of wolves. They look like wolves. They act like wolves with their mortal fights for dominance within the pack. They hunt to kill and eat, though not if I'm around to stop them. They howl together in the haunting song of wolves.

And my kids play with them like friends. They've never bitten a person. They've saved my life in blizzards and on ice that has suddenly given way to deep water.

The sled dog is conversant in two worlds: the human and the wild. They've proven many times that they know game trails and storm patterns and the ways of the woods more insightfully than I. They've also shown that they understand me better than I can, which I see as a form of compassion, of empathy and love. Once the grizzled old leader, Norton, got something caught in his throat after returning from a fast sled run. He couldn't breathe. As I banged in alarm on his chest trying to dislodge the obstruction he stared up at me with a steady, sentient gaze that I know said, "Thanks for trying to help. I've loved you too. If this is it, don't worry." Then he gagged, swallowed, breathed, and got up wagging his tail without further to-do, reassuming his role as "just" dog.

In return I can only look to them to remind me that there is a universe of other realities besides the human. And I can only begin to imagine what their inner life is like.

It's that imagining, though, that opens doors to what's outside my own head.

ΛΛΛ

On a trip to Anchorage I was greeted by a friend, in his fluorescent-lit downtown office, with, "I talk to my dogs now."

I said that he should start paying attention to what they answer.

"I really talk to them," he continued, earnestly. "I talk to them like they're people."

He was intent on making me understand that his hunting dogs had become for him more than silent companions, worthy of articulate conversational speech.

It was odd that he was so determined to convince me. What struck me was not his intensity. Overhanging fluorescence does, after all, irradiate synapses that otherwise wouldn't spark. What I found odd was his implicit suggestion that talking to dogs might be weird.

Talking to dogs is, of course, much healthier and more normal than talking to the television ("Whaddaya mean he was out of bounds!") or talking to cars ("C'mon, baby, turn ovvvvver") or talking to the little beep on telephone answering machines.

I talk to my dogs every day. I only talk to my mother once a week.

I tell Maya how beautiful she looks with her long legs and high carriage. I named her for Maya Plisetskaya, the last of the great Bolshoi prima ballerinas. I tell Mischa how sweet he is, how gentle and childlike in his love; he licks my face and wiggles. If I'm talking to Dick or Bruno I tell them that they're looking tough, which is unavoidable because of their fighters' scars and gnashed noses. They like to look tough. They think Maya likes tough. Maya, however, does not like tough anywhere near as much as she likes not getting pregnant again. I try to explain that to Dick and Bruno but they don't believe me.

I even talk to the lead dog Norton without speaking. He knows what I'm thinking. I'll go outside to get a piece of firewood, look at the clearing sky, think, "Maybe I'll take the dogs for a run," and suddenly Norton is on his feet barking plaintively, crying, "Yes! Now! Let's go!"

The reason that talking to dogs is easier and more rewarding than talking, say, to a two-year-old ("No! Daddy said no. N.O. No. I know you understand me. Hey! Stop already! NO!") is because dogs do understand and are eager to please.

Inanimate objects like televisions and cars and the IRS do not understand. Other animals like cats might understand, if they feel like it, but they are not eager to please.

A girlfriend in New York City once had a cat called, typically, "My Love." One summer day it wandered out the open fifth-floor window to explore the pigeon droppings on the window ledge. My girlfriend went into hysterics. "My Love!" she cried. "Come back to mommy!" The cat looked at her, saw her distress, and looked away. When she reached for it the cat pulled back, and fell. It landed in a mailman's twin-bagged pushcart. The mailman, being a New Yorker, just lifted it out and dropped it on the sidewalk.

My dogs play head games with me, too, but not arrogant,

hell-with-you games. On hard slow freight runs they'll malinger, innocently but transparently. They don't want to struggle up the tundra dragging a quarter-ton load, and I sympathize. When they begin tugging halfheartedly, no matter how I cajole from behind the sled, pushing and panting, I get in front of them. I walk a little way, turn and whistle, and with renewed enthusiasm they pull hard again.

I don't know why they see me as more of a team member—trying to help—when I'm walking in front of them rather than pushing hard from behind, but they do. It might be because leaders work the hardest, and the rest of the dogs follow the example of the leader, even if the leading is only trudging ahead to show that movement is possible.

These dogs love to pull. They're athletes, always glad to practice their sport. When we finish a hard run they are unmistakably proud. We carry on a complete articulate conversation:
"How's that, boss? Solid, huh?"

"Yeah, good job, guys."

"Don't we always make it? Have we ever given up?"

"You're the best. The very best."

"Got that right. Now let's have some extra food."

"Sure. Coming up."

"Thanks, man. Love you, dude."

"Love you, too."

Without them we wouldn't live where and how we do. We probably could, but it would be an enormous effort. They know it. I don't even have to tell them. But I do. Often.

That's not weird. It's respectful.

ʌʌʌ

The alternative to dogs for maintaining a remote homestead is a lot of machines. A snowmachine for winter, a balloon-tired all-terrain vehicle for summer, a full tool shop for grinding, welding, boring, and patching the snowmachine when it breaks down, which it will, often.

Look at the Inupiaq people of Alaska's Arctic Ocean coast. They've been running dogs since forever. Given the choice between a good dog team and a new snowmachine, what will they now choose nine times out of ten?

A new snowmachine.

I figure that if I'd been running dogs since forever I'd get a kick out of a sixty m.p.h. hot rod, too.

Fact is that the Arctic Ocean coast is wide open: no trees, no winter brush, no firewood to haul, lots of Prudhoe Bay oil tax money to burn.

In the upper Su Valley the physical and economic world is so different that dogs win over machines paws down. At least, that's my conclusion.

We keep between seven and ten big dogs. The cost for dry food in commercial fifty-pound bags is a little more than a thousand dollars a year. Additional expenses include harnesses and line, wormer and vaccination shots. All of it comes to about a fourth the cost of a standard snowmachine.

A machine, of course, requires gas and oil and spare parts and a pair of special tubular snowshoes to strap on the back of the seat for the inevitable breakdown way the hell out somewhere without the proper tools to make repairs.

We bring in all our supplies with the dogs—windows for the new bedroom addition and firewood. We travel to the mountains with the dogs. They're not as fast as a new machine, but the time spent coming and going is serene. It's impossible to hear the forest above an engine's scream. After any length of time straddling a machine one's body continues to vibrate when the motor's finally been turned off.

We count on the dogs in the summer, too. They keep bears away from the house clearing. When we go to the road we often travel the two or three miles down the flowering tundra by sled—dogs panting in the heat but glad for the exercise. When we then chain them in the shade of the forest so we can hike the rest of the way we put a dogpack on one or two of the stronger dogs. They'll carry twenty pounds apiece.

The summer alternative is an all-terrain vehicle—four-wheel-drive, giant-tire golf carts with attitude. ATVs should be banned from the back country. They decimate tundra. They rip up the earth.

I once believed that the perfect number of dogs to keep was six. All my musher acquaintances chuckled at my small lot. If I ever wanted to race, they said, I'd need a minimum of twenty more dogs. Fifty dog lots are common. They assumed it was just a matter of time before I wanted to race.

Sled-racing dogs come in three sizes: medium, small, and ridiculous. Sprint dogs are the smallest; long-distance dogs (as for the 1,000-mile Iditarod Race) are the "largest." They are all bred to go go go go go go. If I wanted to race, I'd get a snowmachine. In fact, I'd have to get one. I know no dog racers who do not have at least one snowmachine, to "groom" their trails. Sled dog races all follow snowmachine trails. Dog racers complain when the snowmachines out in front don't pack the snow well.

Eight dogs is now what I see as the perfect number. Eight bear-chested, jaguar-legged, all-terrain huskies. I've been out on solo expeditions for a month with eight dogs. The dogs and I have made our own trail. Trips like that are impossible with any machine. Convoys of machines would probably work. But then, being in the wilds would be pointless with that kind of mess.

The dogs reveal much about the landscape we travel through: new routes, concealed wildlife, hidden crevasses, the joy of being out in the silence of the woods, which they feel, too. Machines are faster. So what?

///\

The invention of the spear was probably accidental: Some clutzy caveman stepped on a stick that snapped up into his face. He grabbed the sharp piece, heaved it angrily, and watched as it then buried itself in an old tree trunk, quivering.

Or the deadfall: An early trapper bent over to yank a long

root from the trail, heard a whistling sound, and looked up just in time to see a tree falling toward his head.

Here what we've discovered: When we ran the dogsled in summer down the carpet of the tundra and reached the woods at the far end, the dogs didn't stop when I stepped off the sled where they should have stopped. They smelled something, and ran on. I chased them into the forest, calling my special husky command ("Damnit! Whoa! Goddamnit!"), until they decided to stop to take turns pissing on a trail-side tree. I was so annoyed I jumped on the back of the sled and snarled, "OK, you want to crash through the woods? Let's go."

So they did. And it was great.

Here's the song we made up after trying that discovery a few more times:

Hooking up the dogs on a sunny fall day
No snow on the ground but we're on our way
We're flying
Over roots and stumps
We're flying
Gonna take our bumps
We're flying
It's just WHOAAA! and then *thump.*

We have destroyed two sleds beyond the point of repair by driving the dogs down the forest trail when there's no snow to cushion the course. But we haven't busted bones.

The trick is to hook up as few dogs as possible to go without hooking up too many to control. The places in the trail where large roots of trees are exposed are like skids under logs: the sled runners slide over them quickly. The muddy places in the trail give a respite from the white-knuckled parts.

We don't run the sled often when the summer brush is at its height because it's too difficult to see what might be just ahead: bear, bull moose, newly fallen tree. If we ever ran smack into a sow with cubs the scene is too grotesque to dwell on. But lining the sled with second-hand couch cushions and enthroning a young boy inside is a more fun way to travel than plodding with half-steps behind a kid who keeps pausing to ask, "How much farther? Will you carry me again?"

"In the summer traditional peoples of the Arctic turned the dogs loose to forage for themselves," says a history book in our library.

Our dogs have a better time leaping down the summer trail in the joy of running, knowing that they'll eat better when we get home than if they'd forage for themselves.

⋀⋀⋀

Winter in the upper Su Valley can be defined less by temperature than by the temperament of the resident mushers. When they become serious, winter has arrived.

They have less time for small talk. Any conversation that doesn't revolve around dogs is too small to consider. They organize their lives around training for upcoming races, not around mundane things like eating or sleeping.

A few years ago, during the heyday of the local Moose Creek 300 Mile Sled Dog Race (the equivalent of a rural county softball tournament) the race added "International" to its name because a Frenchman came all the way from France to train for it. That was how we described Tony: A Frenchman from France, as if needing to reiterate the unusual truth of someone giving up Chateaux Margaux, *foie gras,* and urbanity for dog shit in the woods.

Tony was *seriously* serious. He rented a little log hovel across from the Moose Creek Tavern and then, for two months, refused to drink even one glass of wine. A Frenchman who refused wine! He was in training. The dogs he bought upon arriving in the area were in training. He had followed his dream to race a dogteam in Alaska, and nothing was going to distract him. He didn't even pursue women, which didn't take much fortitude since the demographics of this part of the valley overwhelmingly favor men, and dogs.

Tony was an excellent ambassador for the sport. He was dedicated to his team. And he gave up wine and women for it.

The upper valley is renowned in Alaska for dogsled training because of its long snow season. Locals who had not before imagined themselves as dog drivers began to think twice. The convivial owner of the Moose Creek Tavern got himself a starter team not long after Tony arrived. With visions of smoothly streaking through the woods behind a silently loping team, Lon harnessed his three new dogs and set out.

He stood in the snow-plowed driveway of the bar on the back of a small sled. One dog curled up under the sled, one yawned and urinated on its foot, the third hysterically leaped about tangling all the lines while Lon, veins bulging on his neck, spittle on his lips, screamed, "Gee! Damnit, GEE!" holding out his right arm like a semaphore in case the dogs didn't remember that "gee" meant "to the right."

Exhibitions like that of mushing technique are why snow-machines are popular. It's also why serious training is so common, to avoid humiliation.

Then again, there are people who have no fear of embarrassment. When my mother first came from Chicago to visit in winter she exulted about the beauty of the forest and the isolation, then cried out, when she'd climbed into the sled to be driven to the homestead, "Moosh, you huskies! Moosh!"

The dogs all looked round to figure out what she was trying to say.

"Uh, mom," I said. "It's 'mush', not 'moosh' and usually we just say 'okay' or 'hike' or just whistle once to get the dogs to go."

Undaunted, she replied, "But I thought it was 'moosh.'"

"No," I said, "no."

"But 'mush' sounds like soggy cereal," she insisted. And 'okay' doesn't have any excitement in it."

"'Mush' is the English corruption of the French-Canadian 'marche': to go," I explained.

We compromised with letting her say anything she wanted to the dogs as long as it was not where anyone I knew could hear her.

Usually, though, what serious mushers say to their dogs is much more emphatic than can be repeated to one's mother.

"I finally realized that all the top mushers have dogs from the same bloodline," said a novice to me. "The surname of the dogs is the same. It's 'Damnit.' There's 'Whoa Damnit' and 'No Damnit' and, of course, the usual lead dog name, 'God Damnit.' It's amazing how many mushers have lead dogs with the same name."

Intensity of expression is all in the pursuit of an excellent team that doesn't cause humiliation. When that's been achieved, when the dogs are all in step running with the speed of the wind at their backs so that the air is perfectly calm around us and snow swirling from the ground rises in slow motion to hang beside the moving sled as if in a bright bubble, then the time for being serious is over.

/\/\/\

She wasn't a bad dog. A distant neighbor, the Professional Mid-Distance Musher, had once wanted to buy her. She wasn't even particularly old, just eight, still able to breed and still glad to pull. She was, in fact, our most obedient dog, a natural sweetheart, never a need for reprimand.

But she was small. The rest of the team had become like a conga line of muscled bears, swift and powerful. And there in the middle, her legs at times windmilling six inches above the ground, would be my little white fox, Puppy Girl.

When I first moved to Alaska I found an abandoned cabin on Dead Dog Ridge. One day I asked my neighbor, Starvin' Marvin, why it was called Dead Dog Ridge. Marvin had been running dogs for years. He was familiar with the gritty side of mushing, the side no one talks about much. In reply to my question he looked me in the eye, patiently, silently. "Oh," I said. "Of course."

What does one do with a vibrant and capable sled dog that has been supplanted by better dogs? Turn her loose to pasture? Helicopter her to a distant valley where she can join a wolf pack?

The traditional answer has been, and remains, the way of Dead Dog Ridge: ka-blam.

But shooting Puppy Girl was inconceivable. She wasn't sick, she wasn't ailing. Keeping dogs on the ends of chains was bad enough.

So I sent Puppy Girl to California. My wife took her along during a visit with siblings. I hoped that a cute white Alaskan husky would make people stop on the street and ask to buy her.

People on the street stopped and asked to buy her. The average amount offered was $350. But my son decided he wanted to keep her when he heard. "She must be good if she's worth so much. Besides, she's sweet."

So back she came. Within six months we'd had another litter and a dog lot of too many. The pups would become sleek and smart and strong.

I took Puppy Girl to the animal control shelter, to see what the chances were that someone would adopt her. The chances were not too good. Alaska has many cute white huskies. So I brought her home, again.

Finally, after a friend had told a friend who told a friend about the dog, Puppy Girl found sled-dog heaven: a big new dog house in a large backyard with an eleven-year old girl cuddling her at night in love.

This ending is exceptional, but a relief. It's a triumph of luck more than perseverance. Responsibility for another's life is an enormous obligation.

But then, we're all responsible for recognizing our inextricable involvement with the intricate web of life.

ΛΛΛ

I shot Dick because he was old and in pain, because he lived on the end of a chain crying to run with the rest of the team but unable to keep up even if loose behind the sled. He would stumble, then, and fall far behind.

I shot Dick because I didn't want to bring him to the pound to be put in a cage for three days and then gassed. My sons grew up with Dick. I traveled across Alaska with Dick, across mountains and glaciers and the frozen ocean. Dick was one of our original dogs who pulled loads into the homestead before there was anything here except forest. He deserved to die in my arms.

But I shot him twice in the head with a 12-gauge, and left him deep in the woods where his body would return to earth.

I'd been postponing his death for a year, hoping to come up with a better solution, one that would be kinder to him and to me. There wasn't one. No one wanted an old ailing dog for a new pet. He cried so mournfully when left behind.

Shooting Dick was traumatic. The worst part was that he knew he was going to die. And he nuzzled me. And lay down. And waited.

Good God.

I don't want that kind of power. I don't know how to handle that depth of love.

Living in a remote part of Alaska certainly requires an intimacy with death. The cycles of life are immediate, unavoidable, constant, and death is inevitable. Sentimentality is often a liability.

When I was a kid I was affected by the classic book *Old Yeller*. It ends with the dog needing to be shot because it had rabies. When the trigger is pulled it's like watching Juliet stab herself beside Romeo's body. Inevitable, perhaps, but overwhelmingly tragic. It isn't fair. It isn't the way things should be. Love should conquer all suffering. Love is the same in both people and animals. Any division between people and animals is false.

The law in Alaska states that a dead animal is "solid waste," like a beer can or an old tire, and must be deposited in a garbage dump. This law is, of course, insane. It's another ghoulish reminder that species other than our own are commonly seen as not worthy of morality, beneath considerations of conscience.

The standard way to end an animal's suffering is to go to a vet, sit under fluorescence atop Formica, and wait for a lethal injection to work. The animal then becomes "solid waste," to be legally disposed of.

Dick lived his life in the woods. Now he's food for ravens and fox and marten and blueberries and lichen.

Solid waste. Where did the people who make such laws come from?

Perhaps Dick knew that it was best for him to die, less painful than continuing to live, less futile. "Many men would take the death sentence without a whimper to escape a life sentence which fate carries in her other hand," wrote T.E. Lawrence. There's no division between people and animals.

But I'm the one who decided he needed to be "put out of his misery." That's what makes his grace as he lay down so difficult to handle. "I trust you to know what's best," he seemed to say. "Love you. Bye."

That depth of love is extraordinarily rare, in any species.

The conventional denouement to this would be Dick's little pup growing up to be just like his dad. In fact, Dick did leave a male sire, but Groucho looks nothing like his father, and has the manic excitability of his mother. Dick was laconic.

Dick's son is, however, an aggressive fighter, like his dad, and gently loving, like his dad, and very sensitive to being left behind, too. When the family that adopted Groucho goes away, the dog cries mournfully.

I heard that sad call the other day. It was chilling. A ghost song.

I spoke aloud to Dick. "We can't go off and leave you anymore, Dick. Now you'll always be with us."

MOUNTAINS AND EXPEDITIONS

The mountains are the dominant force in the valley. They create the weather, the climate, the topography. They define the boundaries both of the valley and of the known. Within the snow mountains remain mysteries.

Glaciologists and geologists and zoologists continue to discover truths about the life processes of and amidst the hills. Adventurers discover truths about themselves.

Expeditions into the mountains are compelling, both for those who travel from distant countries to explore them and for those of us who live beneath them. The root of the word "expedition" means "to bring forward, to make ready," from the Latin *expedire*, which literally is "to free one caught by the foot."

Stepping into the mountains is freeing, certainly, and heightens a quality of attention, of consciousness.

How many religions *haven't* looked to mountains for their revelation? From Greek mythology to Tibetan Buddhism, from Moses to Mohammed, interaction with the divine has always been found where the land meets the heavens.

Dogen, in the thirteenth century, wrote, "Mountains have been the abode of great sages from the limitless past to the limitless present. Wise people and sages all have mountains as their inner chamber, as their body and mind. You may think that in mountains many wise people and great sages are assembled. But after entering the mountains, not a single person meets another. There is just the activity of the mountains. There is no trace of anyone having entered the mountains.

"There are mountains hidden in sky. There are mountains hidden in mountains. There are mountains hidden in hiddenness. This is complete understanding."

ʌﬡʌ

In 1983, when not many living people knew what *was* out in the reaches of the valley, I took my first extended trip into a rarely visited part of the Range. It was the beginning of a sequential exploration of each of the Denali area's five great glacial watersheds, one at a time, one week's-long trip per year, with different partners or alone, traveling by dogsled.

I'd climbed Denali itself two years earlier, during the summer climbing season, but the ascent was by the most common route, among a dozen, from Base Camp. There were almost a hundred other climbers on the mountain at the time, though it seemed that I met no one. From the summit, on an unusually clear day, I could see limitlessly. I studied those five sinuous glaciers descending from the massif to the valley floor. They spanned seventy miles, from the Yentna Glacier past the Kahiltna, Tokositna, and Ruth, to the Eldridge, each glacier winding among serrated snow peaks to finally poke its blue snout into the distant greenery of the summer lowlands. I had not the slightest conception of what there might be amidst that enormous panorama of Mountain. I thought that, in order to understand the area I called my home, I should go see up close.

I first went with a local musher named Michael atop April's

snowcover across the lowland forest toward the Ruth Glacier. We entered the foothills by running up the mostly frozen Coffee River, which the Athabascans called The Creek That Roars (*Betnu Detniyitnu*), evidently for the places at its lower end where it cascaded through boulders, even in winter. We avoided that stretch, following the bank. The Coffee, named by an eighty-five-year-old Talkeetna prospector I'd met in town, ascends through a narrow canyon twenty miles long to reach its small but numerous glacial sources.

Our plan was to try an unnamed pass between unnamed peaks to climb up out of the Coffee, and then to descend immediately to the huge Ruth Glacier, which flanked the river canyon to the south. From there we hoped to travel down the glacier back to the valley floor and on home.

We followed a wolverine track up the canyon toward the pass since, as Michael pointed out, wolverines always take the shortest route. Michael was already a ten-year resident of Talkeetna at a time when the number of people who'd been in the upper valley for more than ten years was perhaps a hundred. He favored wool pants with suspenders, with hand-sewn patches at the knees for reinforcement. He had courted the stories of the real old-timers—the prospectors and trappers who now lived in town, "retired" from their days in the hills during the first Caucasian influx—so when he mentioned that he didn't believe anyone had investigated our route before, I understood that he meant *ever*.

I had been surprised at the amount of wildlife in the canyon of the Coffee. I knew that bears denned there and other similar canyons amidst the glaciated hills. But I hadn't imagined that the mountains could support flocks of a hundred ptarmigan, with tracks of many fox, marten or ermine, and coyote. We saw porcupines, and a dozen moose. One of the moose was dead, caught in an avalanche, a single leg sticking above the snow: a spring bear's breakfast. The vegetation—willow especially—fed moose and ptarmigan. Voles under the snow fed fox and weasel.

This was obviously why "cave" people lived where they did in the Pleistocene. The canyons were rich with life. Even in winter.

When we got to the top of the pass, however, a different world opened. It was the world not of plants and animals, of seasons cycling, of human association. It was so distinct it seemed as if time had been suspended. Nothing we could see would change in our lifetimes.

Below and beyond and above were quartz and granite and ice and snow, for eons. The glacier itself was almost five miles wide, and it seemed small in the expanse of sheer rock faces and white spires. The deepest gorge on the terrestrial planet, dwarfing the Grand Canyon, was directly beneath us, filled with blue ice.

Behind where we'd just come were alder and willow, water pipits dipping at open leads where the creek flowed, predator and prey tracks criss crossing in the snow. Ahead was a luminous asteroid realm.

We followed the glacier for days back down to the valley floor, making long detours around crevasses, waiting out snowfall so thick it was futile to try to see an arm's length ahead. When we first smelled trees again (suddenly, after cascading fifty feet down a snow slope off the glacier, dogs tugging hard toward the spruce and cottonwood grove), it was as if we were accelerating back into time.

My next exploration into the valley's extremities was to the Tokositna Glacier, just south of the Ruth. The Tokositna carved a great amphitheater as it withdrew to its present terminus. Enclosed by mountains, except where the glacier's meandering braided river slices through to the valley floor, that basin is one of the world's major breeding grounds for trumpeter swans. Canada geese and other large migratory birds rise in raucous swarms when disturbed by predatory fox or wolf. Islands of tall cottonwood and dense alder thickets stand amidst the winding channels of the river. In winter, with the vegetation fallen, bald-eagle nests four feet across loom high in the long-limbed branches of the cottonwood, silhouetted against the hills.

The dogs made trail into the amphitheater until the snow got soft and deep. Then I snowshoed ahead of the team. Weather is a very local phenomenon in the snow mountains, changing dramatically not just across brief intervals of time but also of space, from one canyon or creek to another, like rooms in a mansion.

We found a channel of the river that had recently frozen over. The snow atop it was firm. I stashed the 'shoes, stood on the back runners of the sled, and let the dogs again lead the way.

We headed on toward the top of the basin. Then the dogs lunged and began running hard. They were following an existing trail. "Moose," I immediately assumed, until I looked.

With anxiety I saw that the track was from Bigfoot, or a yeti. Three feet on either side of a groove that seemed to have been made by a dinosaur-sized river otter dragging itself through the snow were deep, regularly placed holes. The foot prints of a huge spider? What the hell? The only association I had with such prints were ski poles, but the wide central groove was not from skis, and the holes would have required a skier to have arms as long as condor wings.

The dogs, glad for any trail, raced for miles until we reached the last grove of spruce beneath a small tributary glacier leading up toward Denali.

The dogs ran right into that grove, and a towering apparition rose.

It was dressed in an orange jumpsuit.

The dogs began barking wildly.

"Hey!" said the monster. "What a surprise!"

It was a resident local, six-foot-six Dave Johnston, a renowned mountaineer. He held a pair of crampons, in pieces. In the snow around him were two large toboggan sleds, roped together, piled high with gear, an equally large backpack, a harness system for towing the sled behind the pack, and the longest set of cross-country ski poles I'd ever seen.

He was lugging 150 pounds of supplies from his cabin twenty-five miles away in an attempt to reach the summit of Denali in winter. That endeavor was unheard of before, and unduplicated since.

"Hope I can get these crampons to work," said Dave.

His was not a corporate-financed expedition.

We visited for a few minutes until he was satisfied with his gear. It was very cold. It was winter. It was helpful to keep moving. I kept looking up the basin, up the winnowing route he'd chosen, up the visible slopes of Denali, and thinking, "This guy is mad."

Dave, however, was calm and casually exhilarated. He was going alone for the sake of the going, without fanfare, without publicity, his eyes not on a *National Geographic* special or a Rolex endorsement, but on the mysteries waiting.

"I can haul your stuff for a ways in the sled," I offered.

He considered. "No," he said, "no, that wouldn't be fair."

He plunged his enormous ski poles into the snow and dragged himself on.

I wandered the Tokositna basin and surrounding slopes for a few weeks after he left, finding surprising conduits through and among the hills. For instance, Bear Creek rose steeply from the basin to a half-mile-high spring that also flowed in the opposite direction from its hilltop source as Glacier Creek, which ran into the watershed of the Kahiltna Glacier, the Range's largest. The Tokositna Glacier curved around the back side of an imposing foothill—rising sharply to serrated summits—but the middle slopes of that mountain could be traversed (one leg bent on the uphill side, one digging straight into the downhill side) to eventually stand above the Ruth Glacier. Peaks separated one glacier from another. Crest and trough. Tributary ice flows feeding those enormous glaciers were separated by peaks. Trough and crest.

At night in my tent I studied maps by headlamp, tracing both my proximate discoveries and the far route Dave was taking. His course was extreme, climbing from one glacier to another, but it went to the heart. I originally imagined the mountains as a barrier, but they now seemed to spread as a great sea, wildly tossed, yet, with skill, navigable.

The Kahiltna ascends forty-three miles to Denali's highest slopes. I'd seen its origin when I'd summited Denali, but had only glimpsed its distant terminus from the flowing spring between Bear and Glacier Creeks. The year I went into the Kahiltna drainage I stayed low. I traveled with a photographer newly arrived in Alaska. Richard was black-bearded and startled when not just his beard but his eyelashes turned to white frost from his breath vapor in the cold. He had ranged the Tetons in Wyoming, but hadn't experienced so much so deep, so intense. He wanted to shoot not just the Alaska Range's grand scale but the small details, the "haikus of light."

With his eye I saw fall's wind-torn birch leaves embedded in winter creek ice, snow patterns at our feet highlighted in bas relief by blue shadow so that kneeling and staring down returned the same image as I'd seen by climbing to 17,000 feet and staring out. The larger landscape was contained within itself, in microcosm. Summer was visibly encased in winter.

When we saw forty moose herd single file from the terminus of the glacier into scrub willow Richard refused to take a picture. Moose do not herd. Forty in one place is very unusual.

"Some things are best just seen," said Richard.

We stood for a long time watching the boreal caravan, shielding our eyes with a hand from the low sun's glare.

Undulating shadow of moose, sharp shadow of snow, great shadow of mountain.

The eponymous river of the Yentna Glacier drains an

exceptionally large area of the valley, flowing eventually, as all the waterways do, into the Susitna. The glacier itself does not lead up to a pass out of the valley but rather to rock walls. None of the glaciers of the Alaska Range are avenues to the other side, opening the valley to the rest of Alaska.

It seemed intriguing, then, the following year, to explore a route that might have led some of the first people into the valley. Maps said it was possible, though whether it was likely remained to be seen.

A skier from Talkeetna named Keith and I traveled in March for a week to reach the top of the West Fork of the Yentna River. Keith, a mountain bum, had no money, like me, but was fascinated to see what he'd never seen. In the summer of 1906 a heavily financed expedition from New York, attempting to find a route to Denali, had ascended the Yentna by boat and then traveled on up the West Fork by foot and pack horse. Dr. Frederick Cook, Columbia professor Herschel Parker, and painter Belmore Browne pushed into the mountains, hoping to cross the Range to reach a climbable flank of Denali. They couldn't get through.

"...After climbing the hill above us, we could see the rounded sheep mountains of the Kuskokwim (on the far side of the Range). But even at that height the mosquitoes were troublesome....We were weak from hunger and the mountain fell off in numerous precipices, and was covered with dense jungles of twisted alders and devil's-club. We traveled mostly on our hands and knees...."

By dogsled Keith and I attempted not that route from the top of the Yentna, but a nearby route hidden from the 1906 expedition by tremendous boulders. 1954 U.S. Geologic Survey maps showed a creek that wound circuitously among those 100-foot-tall rocks, then rose dramatically between sheer walls to an open basin under the Cathedral Spires of the Kichatna Mountains. From that pass we would be able to cross the Range with ease. If we could get that far.

Our start from my homestead had been delayed by a typical spring dump of perhaps four feet of new snow. When we finally reached that unnamed creek we realized that the heavy snows helped greatly in our hope to ascend the route we'd chosen. Beneath our camp the first night in the creek's narrow canyon we could hear water rushing. The fresh snow created an arcing bridge atop the fast water, a suspended canopy.

The next day, a mile further up, the creek had powered through the snow plug, gouging down the middle of the canyon a channel that then disappeared again beneath us. We had to use an ice axe to cut a ledge along the sloping snow that fell into the current. The dogs in single file pulled the sled past the drop; the sled teetered with one runner on the ledge and one runner over air.

For the next five miles the walls on either side narrowed until they were six feet apart. Avalanches that had fallen off the cliffs 500 feet above us had again buried the creek beneath the snow. We crawled like the 1906 party, but beneath falling shards of shale rather than overhanging vegetation. With our hands we had to sweep the sharp rock from the sled's path.

At the top of the creek a frozen waterfall mandated a pulley system to haul each dog and then the sled up into the basin. We ran on down to the other side of the Range.

Two years later an owner of an Alaskan guiding business showed me 5x7 color prints of the route we'd taken. She'd flown the area in a helicopter, scouting potential routes for her clients.

"This is impassable," she declared flatly, pointing to our creek.

We, too, had learned that, except in a heavy new snow, with luck and an ice axe and climbing rope, no people had entered the valley there, or would likely leave it.

There might be channels between different regions within the mountains, labyrinth possibilities for the initiated who could chart the inner shoals, but this closure remained: the valley was and has always been geologically distinct from the lands beyond it, a complete and bounded ecosystem, and yet connected by wind, stars, and primordial memory to the rest of the earth.

ΛΛΛ

Travel through this country by dogsled is like land sailing. The wood of the sled creaks. Leaning from the port side when the sled rolls starboard or leaning starboard on a roll to port keeps the sled from tipping. When the wind is hard in the face, tack, because that's what the dogs will do instinctively. When the wind billows from behind, run on.

Even the lowlands of the valley create an up and down of ravine and rise, saddle and slope. Only the frozen lakes are flat. In the hills, of course, there is constant flux of terrain.

Where there are trees, dogsled travel is idyllic, because no matter how cold the air, a fire at night is balm. On glaciers or hilltops above treeline, winds make the drill of stopping for the night faster-paced.

First, get the dogs out of their harnesses. The dogs' body heat while running through the snow soaks the harnesses; a harness that turns to ice gets chewed. Sitting in the tent with numb hands trying to thread line through a needle hole to sew is taxing.

Next, chop branches for a fire, or pull them from the sled where they've been carried, or light the gasoline camp stove. Melting snow for water is requisite. Dehydration makes frostbite of man or dog inevitable.

With dinner started, set up the tent against winds, walk back and forth to the fire to dump more snow in the pot. Roll out the pad and bag, keep the fire stoked, add more snow, hug the dogs, search for dry socks in the pack, add more snow. A gallon of water per dog per day is good.

Waiting for the dry dog food to soak and the water to cool provides time to look at the stars and meditate on plastic. My boots are plastic. My underwear is plastic. My parka is gilded in bright plastic. If I get too close to the fire, I melt. Next lifetime

I return to skins and furs. What's ten extra pounds when it absolves the suspicion that I'm just a colorful cartoon crinkling against eternity?

When they've eaten, the dogs set up a howl before curling up in the snow to sleep. The basis of their song is gratitude. At times their song is answered by wolves in the distance.

One of the first rules of wilderness travel is to follow the natural corridors: rivers, open tundra, hillcrests. Animal tracks show that they know the rules.

An alternate rule of wilderness travel is to carry a machete. Crossing from one river channel to another usually means pushing through alders. Bushwhacking. Chopping an avenue for the twelve-foot-long freight sled. Sometimes the sled loaded with 300 pounds is like an icebreaker, rising up the crest of the frozen alder sea and then crashing down as alders crack and snap.

But it beats doing it in summer with the bugs and the rain and the ankle-twisting tussocks and the knee-deep swamps and the burden of a pack snagging on brush.

There is not often a vista in summer. A rain forest can be claustrophobic. But in winter the land is revealed, the routes clear, the traveling buoyant.

∧∧∧

We followed an old snowmachine track until it veered in a tight circle and returned on itself. The dogs hesitated. My oldest son, at age 11, driving his own sled, caught up to me so that his lead dog's nose stuck between my knees. We stopped to give the dogs a break before taking them further up the basin.

I was surprised that someone on a snowmachine had come so far, but snowmachines had been quickly increasing in technological capacity in recent years. I hoped the rider had ridden slowly through the trackless snowscape, stopping often simply to look.

Suddenly a pair of trumpeter swans lifted from an open lead

in the frozen river ten yards in front of us. The swans rose, laboring, until they hit a column of dawn sun slicing between the amphitheater's peaks.

Then they burst from blue-white to a gold so radiant that each slow downbeat of wings seemed to shower droplets of light, as if the light covering them was liquid. In the morning mountains it was breathtaking.

Snow still five feet deep on all the world. Air temperature at zero before the heat of the sun. Swans on the wing. No other people. Only trailless wilds ahead.

"These are the good old days!" I called to my son when the swans had flown.

He didn't understand quite what I meant. Nothing was old. Everything was new.

I didn't know if I could explain to him in a way he'd grasp that when he took his kids here he might have to wave to other visitors and make conversation, listen to the drone of snowmachines or ski lifts. It wouldn't necessarily be bad, but it would be completely different.

I tried to hold the moment in memory so that it would always be immediate. "Preserving a moment" is impossible. I felt like an addict helpless to stop reaching for my fix.

Mountains belong to no one, to no memory or hope. Wild land is not in the realm of human beings nor heavenly beings. Viewing it from the scale of human thought only reduces it. Such beauty can't be kept, only noted, like miracle.

"I'm getting cold," said my boy.

We whistled the dogs into a trot and immediately burst into sun.

/\/\/\

There is a *wild* storm atop Denali. The upper half of the mountain is obliterated by what looks like an avalanche moving sideways. It's snow being blasted off the higher slopes. The rest of the sky is clear.

That cloud is streaming out at least ten miles, because I've just checked my map of the Range, and that long roiling banner extending beyond Mount Silverthrone means...

Well, I can't really imagine what it does mean. Who can know what a wind is like that holds snow parallel to the ground for ten miles? It is likely 200 miles per hour and continuous, not just gusting: the jet stream dipped to earth. And it's been blowing all morning.

A storm is classified a hurricane when the winds reach seventy-three m.p.h. I've been in one, and it was extreme.

But up on the summit is incomprehensible.

Down where I sit at my window the sun is making the last of the snow drip from the roof. It's a quiet spring day, with chickadee song.

If that storm were blowing here my house would be pressed flat against Bunco Hill nine miles away. The only thing streaming would be the dogs, flapping at the ends of their chains. The trees to which the chains are affixed would have been snapped off about mid-trunk.

If that storm blew through Anchorage all the cars on cross streets would be tumbling end over end, every small plane parked at an airstrip would be airborne on a final kamikaze flight, pieces of glass from shattered windows would cut down anything standing outside, most if not all buildings would become "outside."

The sustained intensity of that kind of storm has never been recorded anywhere near sea level. As far as I know it's never been recorded anywhere except the upper slopes of Denali. It is not that unusual there, either.

In 1967 all the members of a climbing party who got caught above 17,000 feet were blown to oblivion. Another expedition estimated the windchill temperature in a similar storm to be 148 degrees below zero. A finger held up in such cold to test the direction of wind would be snapped off about mid-digit.

On a calm day I can see the creases in Denali's face. Often that face seems imperious—the result, I assume, of having lived 500,000 years. Occasionally I see an expression of serenity, which would come from retaining the long clear gaze of detachment while the rest of the visible world changed utterly. To weather a storm such as now blows without having a wink altered—and to have weathered countless such storms—commands a respect that quickly becomes humility.

The storms of human history are paltry compared to the power up there.

When the winds slow and the summit is again revealed, it will look as it always does, and will, for as long as people stare up.

∧∧∧

Thank God it's over.

Denali has finally been climbed alone in winter successfully, which means both "to the top" and "without dying."

It's been a sweepstakes the last few years. Strong men with heavy loads have slogged toward the top hoping for the luck to claim first place. The last brass ring of fame for first ascents on Denali has been to do it alone in winter.

Naomi Uemara, a Japanese hero who had climbed Everest and driven dogs to the North Pole, summited Denali solo in winter, but died coming down. Local resident Dave Johnston made the first up and down in winter, but along with a party of others, and then when he tried alone years later, turned back when he frostbit his feet already damaged in his first winter climb. So, by the rules of western civilization's competitive ethics, their solo achievements win no prizes.

The great majority of summer climbers who don't make it to the top fail because of weather. Plainly, the weather is a lot worse in winter. But just as plainly it was inevitable that someone would luck through to the front page.

After all, the Inuit people of the Arctic coast have been surviving extreme winter weather for millennia. And they've done it historically without goose-down bags and Gore-Tex parkas and freeze-dried Lobster Newburg and airplane drop-off, pick-up, and resupply.

The fact remains that Denali in winter can have much stronger winds than the Arctic coast, but exposed flesh knows no difference between 100 below and 140 below. A snow cave at any temperature is just as cozy.

Denali does, however, have crevasses and the dangers of high altitude. And the upper Arctic has sudden openings in the ocean ice and the dangers of polar bears.

The biggest difference between climbing Denali alone in winter and hunting alone on the Arctic ice in winter is that our civilization thinks it's a big deal to have done a big adventure, and the Inuit civilization simply did it.

What mattered most to traditional Eskimo culture was heart, the spiritual heart of being where it mattered. What matters to traditional Western culture is conquest. And the ensuing endorsements.

There was once a time when people climbed mountains to see visions. They went to wrestle with angels where lightning struck.

Exodus 19:20: "…and the Lord called Moses to the top of the mount; and Moses went up." He did not go to bag a first ascent.

How come the Japanese for Fujiyama and the Balinese for Agung and the Ceylonese for Sri Pada and the Tibetans for the entire Himalaya and the Masai for Kilimanjaro and the Incas for Aconcagua and the Aztecs for Popocatapetl and the Navajo for Ship Rock have no record of who made it to the top first? Because it didn't matter.

Revelation mattered.

Most of the world's great mountains are approached and climbed to varying altitudes by people who go to see and not to conquer. Where are their names and the eager articles about them in the media?

Here, for one: Ephraim M'Ikiara. In 1978, at age fifty-two, carrying only a thin blanket, a piece of hemp rope, a small bag of food, and a Bible, he climbed 17,022-foot Mount Kenya, barefoot. When a typical plastic-equipped Western mountain climbing expedition offered assistance during his descent, he replied, "Was it you who showed me the way here?"

The expedition took his picture and recorded his name. Naturally, they didn't draw out M'Ikiara's explanation of what had compelled him, of what devils and gods he had confronted alone at the heights. "Because no one else had done it barefoot carrying a Bible," was not his motivation.

Mallory's historic explanation, "Because it is there," is not a sage bit of Zen wisdom. It's inarticulate egotism.

So now that we're sure Denali can be climbed alone in winter will there be a rush of new solo expeditions to follow the route? Hardly. It's "been done."

But we will inevitably see the First Woman's Solo Expedition. And maybe the First Oldsmobile Ascent (fuel by Amoco, tires by Goodyear).

Then, after the last first ascent has succeeded, and there are no other "firsts" to record, we might start hearing other reasons for climbing mountains other than to blare.

The tin bugles of fame, glory, and victory will be silenced in favor of whispers of *koviashuktok,* an Arctic coast Inuit concept meaning "full awareness of the present moment and place, with great joy and without desire."

ʌʌʌ

I'm atop Long Peak, a domed foothill of alpine tundra and lichen-colored scree in the Denali massif.

A mile below, a silver river winds among cottonwood gold and willow bronze. Across the gorge, sharp peaks of dark rock are studded by small blue hanging glaciers. Denali itself, like the full moon fallen to earth, white and glowing, covers the horizon.

A red-tailed hawk is hanging almost motionless on currents not far from where I sit, cocking its head this way and that. The sound that floats up from below is like ocean surf.

What is most striking is not the view but the light amidst it, on it, within it. It's an early fall day after rain clouds have cleared. The air is washed pure, the north breeze crystal.

Each hair on the back of my hand, as I write, is prismatic, like eyelashes look when squinting into the sun, but vividly distinct, each hair wavering in the breeze. It's as if I was peering through a microscope, seeing unfamiliar but recognizable pattern.

The pieces of rock scattered beside me seem alive. Some are like tiny new volcanic islands with waves of green and russet moss curling up over their shore, some are splotched with intensely black and yellow and red lichen so thin the growth seems to have no texture of its own, like watercolor.

The rock pulses. It *moves,* oscillating, first a little closer then a littler further away. It's like a small forest animal caught in a spotlight, rooted to its spot but trembling.

"You should not remain bewildered and skeptical when you hear the words, 'Mountains flow,'" said Dogen. "When you take one view you see mountains flowing, and when you take another view, mountains are not flowing....Accordingly, do not doubt mountains' walking even though it does not look the same as human walking."

Light this intense is like breathing pure oxygen. All senses are heightened. Goethe's last words on his deathbed were, "More light!"

Light can be converted directly to electricity in a panel of silicon chips. Silicon is veined throughout these mountains. Maybe that's where the buzz of being on this hill comes from.

The south face of Denali looks transluminated. The light seems to be coming through the peak, not reflected. It creates a radiance such as medieval painters tried to depict around the heads of saints. Certainly, with so much quartz and silicon layered within the mountain it could be true translumination. Let geologists scoff.

Without much imagination I can see waves of photons streaming from the sun. The tiny dots of color we all see simply by shutting our eyes are pouring from the sun's corona. It gives the light a corporeality that seems appropriate for how dense it feels on my skin. In rarified atmosphere is heavy light.

Once, in the Nevada desert, I felt the same weight of light, as if it could be netted in the air, as if it could be packed like a snowball. I was baffled because I thought of that quality as being a function of elevation, of mountains. The desert, I assumed, was near sea level. Then when I drove down to the next town the population sign also had the elevation: 7,200 feet. Base camp height.

The polar latitudes are where the Van Allen belt curves like a donut to its hole. The belt is where highly energetic cosmic particles are trapped in the magnetic field of Earth. Those cosmic rays from outside the solar system find a clear path to the planet at this latitude. They charge the aurora. They stream into the mountains' crystals. They are not visible to the human eye, but evident in the deep consciousness of cellular affinity.

There is light that can be seen and light that can be felt and light that can be intuited.

With such full illumination nothing can be obscured. Everything is vivid: each glance of a hawk, each rock, each breath.

ΛΛΛ

It's expedition season again. March and April.

The winter's snows have settled. The daylight is lengthening. There are stars in the freezing nights and warm breezes in the sun.

Time to get out the maps, dust off the beaver-hide overmitts, put a new edge on the knife.

Lessons from experience (read: "screwing up") abound. Each lesson makes for greater confidence on the next trip, unless I actually think of how those lessons happened. Then, if I'd learned anything, I'd stay at home and keep the knife dull so I don't accidentally cut myself.

Before making an early exploration, I asked Joe Redington about my planned route when my dogteam and I met him and his dogteam on a training trail. He founded the Iditarod dogsled race from Anchorage to Nome, and continued to run it well into his seventies. He remains craggy and knowledgeable. I had been told he knew the area where I wanted to go. I described it to him.

"Could run a battalion of National Guard tanks up through there," he said.

I looked at my map when I got back home. My map said a mountain goat would be hard pressed to get through. But Old Joe said. So I went. Maps take experience to read well.

At the start of the ascent up the precipitous canyon, I could see small snowslides sloughing down. It was suicidal, an avalanche chute.

I looked at the map for the hundredth time. The test pattern of my consciousness repeated its refrain like a song: "But ol' Joe said...but ol' Joe said..." Then it hit me that Joe was talking about the *other* way into the pass, far distant from where the dogs and my companion and I were. Duh. That way was along the Iditarod trail, a virtual highway. I'd never considered it because it was so common.

My incredible stupidity made me suggest to my partner, with a clarity of communication I obviously lacked in talking with Joe, "Let's go back."

My partner was childless and unmarried. "What are you, a *wuss?*" he snapped.

I wasn't familiar with the word, but I knew the tone. I thought the word could mean "a highly intelligent and stalwart man who would never jump off a high cliff just because everyone else was doing it."

"Yep," I said. "Uh-huh, you bet, yessir, that's me."

But the howling wind carried away my reply as my partner started up.

After many near-death experiences (such as cutting frozen cheese in my lap with numb hands and a sharpened knife) we eventually arrived at a trap-line cabin used as a checkpoint for the Iditarod. The race had gone through (leaving 1,600 dogs' worth of shit and piss around the cabin), but inside was a left-over case of M&Ms.

Is eating twenty or thirty packs of M&Ms at once as reward for a hard crossing as dumb as reading a map with tunnel vision? I had lots of time to debate the question as I squatted in the vast open-air outhouse.

The first time I teetered at the top of a mountain pass with the dogs eager to pull the sled a half-mile almost straight down I knew what to do.

"Rough-lock the runners" is a great phrase. It has that hard core, casually competent sound, like "trim the ailerons."

I turned the sled on its side and wrapped chains around the runners, clipping them off to the stanchions. Then I wrapped extra polypropylene sled line around the runners, just to make sure.

With plenty of drag now so the sled wouldn't overtake the dogs and crash, I stood on the back, held on tight, and shouted, "Let's *go!*"

The dogs lunged and immediately jerked back, some falling on their butts. The sled didn't budge. The snow was quite a bit wetter and stickier than I'd thought. The slope was south facing, in sun. We'd ascended in shadowed cold from the north.

Frustrated at the time spent rough-locking the runners and at my miscalculation, I started shoving the sled to the bottom while the dogs strained. My traveling companion, stationed half-way down with his 16 mm movie camera to record my historic plunge, used up a lot of film.

The next morning, from our camp at the bottom, I went back up with the dogs to get the cache of supplies we'd left at the pass. The trail I'd made had frozen during the night. I didn't rough-lock the runners. The ride down was so fast and so frightening that it felt like we were in free fall.

It was in the age before camcorders, so an old home movie would only have shown a silent plummeting blur, without the Doppler-effect sound of a long scream.

When a guy I know got himself in a perilous situation—stormbound and lost in the mountains without food—loved ones feared the worst.

"Malcolm" (identity bracketed to veil his screw-up) survived by actually eating one of his sled dogs. I'd never known someone to resort to that survival technique.

"Malcolm," while waiting out the storm, was embarrassed to think that there would probably be rescue parties looking for him. His chagrin was because he is, basically, extremely competent, and had no intention of dying, or of staying lost.

That's the survival technique everyone I know has utilized in perilous situations: adamant pride and absolute refusal to wind up a headline. "Dork Adventurer Drops Dead," is too humiliating to imagine.

Every guy I know in Alaska who takes risks to explore has found himself, at one time or another, in a perilous situation. It's almost a code, an ethic.

But to then actually *die*...that would be like drowning in a bathtub, like getting a five-gallon can of pork'n'beans stuck over your head and suffocating, like using a crevasse for a latrine and toppling in. Instead of returning to loved ones with a story of death-defying deeds that only become more death-defying with each new telling, those loved ones would have to explain, sniffling and bursting into sobs, "And then when he went to wipe himself he lost his balance."

It's no different for them to explain, "He was stormbound

in the mountains without food in a situation so perilous that only great strength and quick wits could have pulled him through, and he dropped dead."

"Rob" was climbing solo in the Talkeetna Mountains, broke an ankle in a fall, and crawled twenty miles to rescue. "David" got trapped in a windstorm on the western Arctic tundra, and for twelve hours leaned his back like a buttress against the nylon fabric of his tent to keep it from shredding. "Denny" was once deep in the Yukon Territory's Mackenzie Mountains, ate some bad rabbit meat he'd snared to survive, got violently ill for days, and still made his way out.

Lesser men would have died.

But none of the people I've known in those or similar situations would ever accept death by default.

The closest to dropping dead I've heard about was when "Rick" woke in the night to the sound of his custom-made canvas winter expedition tent tearing. He was in the mountains overlooking the coastal plain of the Arctic National Wildlife Refuge. The almost hurricane-force winds (as he found out later) had scoured all the snow from beneath his tent before then ripping it, so there was nothing to dig into for protection.

He put on all his clothes, burrowed back in his bag, and clutched his Emergency Locator Transmitter to his chest, scared witless. When the tent blew apart he planned to roll up in a piece of canvas and touch off the radio beacon to bring the Canadian Air Force swiftly to the rescue. He'd registered his emergency frequency with them, the closest source of help.

Then it occurred to me—I mean, him—that only an idiot would think anybody or anything could fly through such a storm. The headline loomed: "Emergency Beacon Brings Chopper to Dork's Frozen Corpse."

No way.

With extra line the pyramid-shaped tent was lashed around

from the outside, the tear held together from within, and with luck the winds began to slow.

/\/\/\

When I go out on a long winter expedition I plan methodically. I bring extra this and that and then some. I don't know what to expect, and so try to anticipate everything, as much as I can. That mentality is flawed. The one thing—or the two or six—that I didn't expect to happen will happen. I'm thrown. I try to compensate, sweating and scheming.

The result is that I'm in conflict with my situation and the land. I don't often accept what's happening. I fight it. Because I'm not yet dead, I've so far won. The effort has been large.

This approach is called: Western.

There's another method. It doesn't try to plan for every possibility. It accepts the truth that the most unexpected thing will happen sooner or later: not a single caribou appearing along a traditional migration route, the little screw holding the spritzle to the sprocket of the snowmachine falling off, the earliest breakup in oral history.

The result of acceptance is presence of mind, immediate adaption. Shock and panic play no part, because there has been no original expectation.

This approach is called: different. It's the manner of wolves and bears, of "prehistoric" people, from whom everyone on the planet is descended. It assumes great faith and greater grace. It allows constant clarity, unfogged by calculations of schedules and odds, unimpeded by an insistence on how things "should" be. It is not a computer mentality. And it seems to have been effective for our forebears, who carried no spare parts.

A Nunumiat Eskimo of an Arctic mountain village has a relationship to the land that is as different from that of most urban dwellers as a wolf's relationship to the land is from mine. I've met extremely competent trappers in the high Arctic who have actually set off on their snowmachines with *maybe* enough gas to complete a complicated trapline loop.

I can't presume to speak for them. I can only speak for difference.

It's plausible to view running out of gas as an inevitability, whether because of a hole in the tank or extra miles ridden to get around an avalanche, just as a snowmachine breaking down without the proper part handy is inevitable. That doesn't rationalize setting out without an extra gas can. But it does extend the pre-trip concentration beyond mechanics. It puts attention while traveling less on the dashboard than on the land.

What happens en route happens. My usual response to complication is a quick "Oh no," followed by an adrenalin-fueled calculation of possibilities. My fundamental desire seems to be to maintain my world, to limit the variability in that world. I sure don't want to stand open to the complexity of the universe when I've got enough immediate complexity to manage.

The only time I respond differently is when the situation is extreme. Then I seem to adopt a different style, instinctively.

I was clambering up a slope to get out of a canyon on a hike-away-from-camp in the Denali foothills. The way I'd wanted to go was blocked by a frozen waterfall. The side slope was not too steep, loose rock covered with powder snow. But it kept on going, getting steeper. I stuck the snowshoes I'd been holding as I climbed between my pack and back, to free my hands for holds. I scrambled higher. The top was not where it should have been. It was up an almost vertical pitch.

I clung to the wall, which began to crumble beneath me. I couldn't go down without sliding. If I fell I'd probably break my back. I *had* to accept the situation. Planning was useless. Presence of mind became instinctive. My awareness turned from off to high.

When I got to the top I couldn't explain how I'd done it. I had seemed to know where to find the firm holds and where the face would pull away. For hours after, I was particularly alert, but I wasn't adrenaline pumped.

I was aware that my thoughts were not along the lines of, "I need to remember to bring an ice axe next time I walk anywhere in the hills." I was aware, instead, of the subtleties of terrain, of each step, of the simple fact that I possessed, as we all do, latent abilities that have nothing to do with brute strength or intellectual discernment.

∧∧∧

The upper Susitna Valley is accessible wilderness. The Brooks Range is as remote as wilderness gets.

The 700-mile-long mountain chain near the top of the planet is entirely above the Arctic Circle. The Alaska public library system has, in its card catalog, forty-one listings under "Amazon," one-hundred and thirty for "Antarctica," but only five for "Brooks Range."

"This is the best description you'll find," said the librarian in Anchorage's comprehensive Alaskana library as she handed me one of those five books, Robert Marshall's *Alaska Wilderness: Exploring the Central Brooks Range*. It was written fifty years ago.

The Gates of the Arctic National Park and the Arctic National Wildlife Refuge (ANWR) are both amidst the Brooks Range. "Essentially untouched," is the way the official management plan of the Gates describes its lands.

I traveled through the central Brooks Range after becoming familiar with the margins of my valley. My partner, who has paddled a kayak down the poorly mapped southern coast of Chile, was as eager to see the Brooks as I was. "There's no deeper wilderness," he said. I approached the trip as if it were a pilgrimage.

For the first two weeks the temperature didn't rise above thirty below. We went up the North Fork of the Koyukuk between Boreal Mountain and the Frigid Crags, then through the Valley of the Precipices.

We crossed over the Arctic divide, the crest at which waters north flow to the Arctic Ocean and waters south to the Yukon River. Trees ended there, too. White mountains, blue shadows, and the hoof prints of caribou were all we could see.

We found deep wilderness pervasive.

But what I had not anticipated, what affected me far more powerfully than the extent of the isolation, was the feeling I had of unity, of interconnection with all the rest of the world. It was the sense I occasionally had in traveling the far corners of the Susitna Valley.

Yet even in the Brooks Range, I could not escape, no matter how hard I tried, the awareness of that land's indivisibility from the ocean north and the rivers south, its connection with the history of men and mammoths and even, once, dinosaurs. All lands have always been connected, like the moon to the seas, like the seas to the shore.

Nor was *I* separated from anything. I had gone to the farthest corner of the earth, and I was acutely conscious of being a part both of those mountains and the valley in which I live, a part of both the natural and the human worlds, of *everything*.

The essence of wilderness, it seems, is not its distinction from anywhere else, but its unity with everywhere else. I couldn't feel like I was in some inviolate realm removed from humanity. The arcing trail of a transpolar jetliner six miles overhead looked like a strand of yarn binding the planet. The countless radio waves and microwaves and cosmic rays streaming through the vault were unavoidable, here, anywhere. Sadly, too, was the sense of atomic fallout from Chernobyl and other nuclear experiments dusting the land, ultraviolet radiation streaking through the damaged ozone, industrial pollution from Siberia and Scandinavia and Chicago tingeing the margins of the sky.

Wilderness does not offer a respite, a reprieve, an escape from encroaching sorrows. Wilderness is a reminder that there is no separation from any problem *there* and an assumed absolution *here.* Wilderness reveals the sky, the rivers, the foundation on which life is grounded, which joins what seems divided.

Everything is of a piece, and has always been. Ignoring that, forgetting it, is the root of much travail, of enormous suffering, of devastation.

When I returned home, I saw my valley as smaller and more fragile, but also as unified with all the edges of the earth.

THE WIDER VIEW: CHANGE AND CONTINUITY

Imagine *being* the valley.

Glaciers send pure water steadily through your veins. Some of that meltwater has been frozen for epochs, molecules held static so long they now race along with wild energy, ions freed.

Nourishment swirls amidst that blood, the dust of ages. The Susitna River makes a sound audible to every boat on it, to every fisherman on its banks. It's the sound of pulverized mountain peaks grating. The oldest rock becomes the newest soil, layering the land, carrying life.

Trees and grasses create your flesh atop mountain bones. They bind that powdered rock against the winds, adding seasonal fertility.

Recently parasites have arrived. Though insignificant individually, they have enormous effect in numbers, like bacteria. They open holes like wounds. They cut swaths through forests, disturb the water table with dams and seeping poisons. From the time of your birth no other presence has been as swiftly and strongly felt.

You know there is much beyond you, beyond the mountains that made and sustain you. You feel tremblings in your guts, the shifting of tectonic plates. Wind-blown spores of distant life settle on your skin. When the sun is constant song erupts everywhere and then diminishes with the return of the stars.

With the weight of ice a mile thick burying everything beneath it recently lifted, the isostatic rebound, as geologists say, continues to raise the valley buoyantly toward the sun. How can that not induce joy? Molecules of everything—organic or inorganic, cellular or crystalline—thrive on energy.

Can the valley be alive, an entity in itself?

If the planet is, which only intransigent ignorance denies, then so too can its parts.

I choose, at times, to imagine the valley not as a rock and water setting for flora and fauna, but as a being-in-itself. If the valley is *like me,* then I find myself unable to do what I unconsciously do often: distinguish *me* from the place I exist, separate my mind from my body, soul from flesh. Subatomic physics now laughs at the archaic notion of individuated and isolated *anything.* Everything is swirled together in such complexity that dim insistence on ultimate division (black from white, now from then, here from there) is absurd.

The first photos from the moon of the blue and silver sphere of our planet didn't make me search for Alaska in the oddly inverted geography. My only thought, staring at the world, was, "That's us, that's *me.*" It was a watershed moment, *getting* the fact that any separation between myself and the earth was just fabrication. I am made of the earth, as is rock and tree and bird. Even if I flew to the moon, I'd be carrying along the elements of the earth that are me.

The valley, too, appears in my mind's eye as it looks from on high, from mountain top or banking bush plane. Instead of the black backdrop of space, soaring white mountains make the image of *home* precious, my life amidst it inseparable from its life. Its life is vital, exquisite.

How can my life, or any life, be less, except by insisting on separation and living that sorrow?

⋀⋀⋀

As both government and private sector proposals to alter the valley ebb and flow (but the level of the swell always increasing), the insistence to do *something* with the land is becoming overwhelming.

Denali State Park, like Denali National Park (like the packaged tourist industry, like local "entrepreneurs"), has a scheme to increase its "user days." I asked one of the state's planners, "Isn't it curious that the land in the park is treated as a commodity to be developed, marketed, and then, of course, consumed?"

The official smiled warmly. "That's just like Mother Nature," he said. "She's an economist, too. Nature preserves resources the way interest on principal is spent without using up the principal. We're just managing the resources the way nature would."

This view is, of course, lunatic.

The mechanisms of life both in the valley and on the planet do not work like the Federal Reserve Bank. Fitting the natural world into simplistic human metaphors ignores the truth that humanity is a part of nature, not a peer, not a supervisor. We've "managed" the grizzlies in Yellowstone to the brink of extinction, "preserved" the Arctic National Wildlife Refuge by clamoring for oil wells.

Hubris is a kind of naive arrogance. Hannah Arendt said that the greatest evil is the most banal, seemingly innocuous, mindless, not consciously malicious.

Hubris is a former governor of Alaska exclaiming, "We can't just let nature run wild!"

Since management is an active rather than passive responsibility, the appointed managers of Denali State Park are not inclined to put their feet up on their desk and say, "The land's perfect just as it is. There's not a single way to improve it." That kind of "manager," in a competitive society, quickly becomes unemployed.

It seems unlikely that the entire cultural paradigm will shift. Hierarchical prerogative is how our society operates. Whether dictatorial or enlightened, whether elected or appointed, some of us manage the rest of us. Overseeing land is easier than supervising people, because it's hard to hear the voice of the land. It's even harder to honor what the land might communicate (if in epiphany and empathy it was heard) should it conflict with our desires.

Certainly the area in the upper valley of Denali State Park is perfect just as it is. Building bridges and roads to the Eldridge Glacier so visitors can snap close-ups of it and high-school kids can party at its overlook isn't necessarily better than reaching it by other means for other reasons. Carving trails with machines and putting up directional signs (Toilet, Keep Left) isn't a higher "use" than exploring wild land on *its* terms.

But fulminating against cultural paradigms is futile.

So look, now, at the vast timber and tundra and glacial watersheds unimproved by any human design. See it as mysterious and alluring and stirring, even without trying to get up close, perhaps just by closing your eyes and imagining its secrets.

Even if port-a-potties and RV dumpsites and roads alter that view, it's what the land is, at least right now, and ultimately will be when the glaciers again descend to wipe the slate clean.

/\\.\\/\\

There have been many ice ages since the decline of the dinosaurs, punctuated by brief interglacials, like now, when human populations increase. The natural warming of the earth between ice ages has been accelerating since the advent of the Industrial Revolution.

The Thames River in England froze solid ten times between 1709 and 1813, but never again. The ten warmest years since reliable instrument records began in the late nineteenth century have all occurred in the last fifteen years, indicating the increasing speed of continued warming.

I could make a case for dramatic global warming from the climate changes in the valley. Fifteen years ago, when I dug the first piling hole for our homestead, the ground was frozen solid. It was June 5. Now, however, by June 5 we're planting in the garden. Forest vegetation comes two or three weeks earlier than I first recorded in my journals.

I'm not suggesting that our homestead's weather "proves" planetary change. The last time I ran the dogs across the high arctic I met a trio of French skiers on their way to the Pole who exclaimed in broken English about the ozone. Their faces spoke most clearly. They were burned purple by the ultraviolet streaking through the damaged atmosphere. I wore a face mask, having learned about fried skin on a similar trip two years earlier.

But the most powerful anecdotal evidence that climate patterns are entering uncharted realms comes from Nome. A conference of Bering Strait Eskimo elders concurred that the seasons are becoming warmer and less predictable. They convened when, for the first time, Norton Sound didn't freeze over in winter. None of the elders had ever heard of Norton Sound not freezing over.

That doesn't just mean in their lifetimes. That means in thousands of years. Oral records passed down through generations are usually highly accurate in cultures that rely on them for life or death decisions. A seventy-five-year-old Yupik-speaking man learned how to read weather patterns on hunts as a boy from men who had firsthand knowledge reaching back to the mid-1800s. Each successive generation has received the distilled wisdom of all that have come before.

Certainly the change in the planet is accelerated by human influence: industrial pollution and forest depletion and the methane farts of cows destined for hamburger. But cataclysmic change in the earth's history has not been uncommon. The number of species becoming extinct this decade—from human intervention or the lack of it—is similar to the number of species that suddenly vanished sixty-five million years ago, when the dinosaurs, too, died out.

There is sizable scientific research, however, showing that not all the dinosaurs became extinct. Some evolved into birds.

I love the idea of the tremendous thunder lizards transmogrifying into song. Dogs howl and bears snort but birds sing. There is no earthly realm where birds have not adapted. Penguins swim like dolphins, ostriches run like cheetahs, condors soar like the clouds.

People, too, now live in most every ecological niche, but not with the same diversity. People tend to forge their habitat, bend and shape it, not adapt to it. Not anymore.

Now we tend to view change as distressing. After all, we've carved our niche.

But whether "natural" or "man-made", whether inevitable or tragic, change is here, and it's happening *fast*.

It would help if those Bering Strait elders, in addition to remembering historic climate patterns, retained and revealed the ancient knowledge of how to soar in trance to flight.

ΛΛΛ

A magazine suggested and then abandoned (on the hysterical "advice" of their attorneys) the idea that I switch homes for a few weeks with a woman writer living where she was raised on New York's Upper East Side. The magazine had originally imagined, I assume, something droll.

"The only water came from a pothole in the ground. The outhouse was unspeakable. But that was trivial hardship compared to blowing on the smoldering kindling of the woodstove through blue lips..." That sort of thing.

I, however, was expecting science fiction.

If a time machine zapped a modern New York City woman back to the Pleistocene, she would turn up in a world almost identical to what most of this upper valley is now. The major difference would be that here there are no wooly mammoths or saber-toothed tigers. She would, however, find hairy cave men.

Academic consensus is that people living in the 1990s A.D. are the same genetically as people living in the 19,000s B.C., when the last glacial sheet still covered what's now Beijing and Paris and Chicago.

A recent book, *The Paleolithic Prescription,* by a trio of Emory University scientists, points out that for 100,000 generations humans were hunter-gatherers, agriculturalists for only 500 generations, industrialized for just ten generations, and computerized for one. They write, "...with genetic makeups essentially out of synch with our lifestyles, an inevitable discordance exists between the world we live in today and the world our genes 'think' we live in still."

This means that if a cave man in skins takes a time machine to modern Manhattan he could easily be shaved, dressed conventionally, and taught to speak the rapid idiom of the street—and no one would notice his difference until he started felling trees in Central Park for a campfire.

But how would a *"Cosmo"* girl fare in the Stone Age? Our homestead drinking water really does come from a mudhole. Our "bathroom" is no less primitive. I throw moose bones I've gnawed to the dogs.

Contemporary global society is proof of our capacity to abandon hunting and gathering to then learn how to irrigate a field or tune a car or diddle a computer—at some level of stress to our instincts.

But can we *unlearn* our hard-won institutional training to resurrect those atavistic skills not used in a classroom or office or city? Can a lifetime of conceiving the world in terms of schedules and data be overridden in order to simply intuit the direction a bull caribou will turn at the confluence of creeks?

In 1904, Vihjalmur Stefansson discovered, in northeast Canada, a community of Eskimos who had never had contact with European civilization. They were, literally, living in a Stone Age without metal pots or metal tools. Stefansson tried to impress them with his rifle. He shot a caribou a hundred yards away. They were, to a man, unimpressed. "Can your magic kill a caribou on the other side of a mountain?" they asked. Stefansson admitted that it couldn't. "Our shaman can kill a caribou on the other side of a mountain," they said, and turned away.

Automated teller machines might seem like magic to us (Presto! Money!), but a "primitive" would find greater magic in touching his harpoon and having a seal rise to the very opening in the sea ice where he waited. Anyone can learn how to use a banking machine, but who knows how to master the powers of intuition?

Like a domesticated dog returned to the wild to starve, it's unlikely that an urbanite would find much ease or sustenance in undomesticated land. And those northeast Canadian Eskimos now live in prefab, electrified towns where many of their children couldn't stalk a seal if their lives depended on it.

The science fiction future has arrived. But to what is it connected, besides a plug?

I once lived at the far north end of Manhattan Island, where dark granite cliffs rise from the Hudson. Below my apartment, across an expressway, there was a strip of undeveloped forest extending for miles along the shore of the river. To reach it required then as now a fast dash across four lanes of highway spinning down from the George Washington bridge.

That small forest is a vestige of the same wilderness the original Indian population called home. I had found, in the course of wandering around down there, a few campsites—not archaeological remains from Iroquois, but the homes of what most urban people would call bums, derelicts, street people. One home was as functional and as…homey…as an Alaska trapper's cabin.

It was built around the hulk of what once had been a Datsun. The shell of the car was roofed with scrap plywood, branches, grasses and bark. Inside the car, which lacked steering wheel or seats, was a foam mattress and sleeping bag. Next to the car were white-painted wrought-iron chairs and tables, the kind usually found on a suburban patio, probably wrestled from sidewalk garbage. There was a garden, a fire pit lined with bricks, an unplugged refrigerator, flower pots of geraniums, and a pile of discarded but utilitarian junk that made it look oddly and charmingly similar to an Alaska homestead. There was even a cache to hold food up off the ground, though it was rigged from bags and not built of spruce.

The highway hummed on pilings above the trees in the near distance. The view was of the forested granitic Palisades across the wide river.

The guy who lived there had chosen the site as an alternative both to the rural Virginia of his childhood and to the city streets, a conscious choice to get the best of both worlds.

Driftwood from the Hudson became firewood. A quarter mile away a spring seeped from rock. Surrounded by twelve million people, this guy had found woodland isolation.

I was reminded that people are everywhere capable of integrating their needs gently into what the land offers. Certainly it's plain that we're adept at mangling forests, trashing coastal plains, and shafting mountain peaks with flag poles.

But we also, just as readily, seek beauty, and find it, without requiring earth-moving equipment.

We fill our little niches with gardens and flower pots. We discover places where we can build fires on the forested banks of great rivers and still have access in minutes to the Metropolitan Opera House, hitchhiking.

Instead of journeying to remote Alaska, some guy found an alcove in an urban arbor, and cultivated it: two worlds overlapping, a fusion of the basic human need to be connected both to people and to the land even in the most unexpected way, but wholly.

There is no difference between our relationship with our spouse, or lover, or best friend, and our relationship to the land.

There is no difference between our relationship to our children, or grandchildren, or stepchildren, and our relationship to the world in which we live.

Intimate relations are extraordinarily hard to live right. They take time, energy, clarity, humility, love. They'd take up our whole goddamned *life* if we let them.

No wonder we try to limit our intimate relationships as drastically as we can. Can you imagine carrying the burden of viewing *all* children as *your* children? Now try to imagine all people as part of your family. Tooooo much. To even suggest that the world itself, the mountains and forests, are like people, like children, just like you, deserving of the same attention and care and love, is exhausting to consider.

If that were true, where would we start?

Actually, the question seems to be: Where do we stop?

We stop where it's comfortable. Isn't the point of modern life to seek greater levels of comfort? Why else have a career if it doesn't pay off?

Starting from the premise, however, that nothing is more important than a connection to that which we love, everything shifts.

Children, instinctively, seek greater levels of connection. Joseph Chilton Pearce, a contemporary philosopher, suggests that human development is a series of bondings to progressively wider worlds: the fetus to its nurturing womb, infant to mother, child to father, to community, to the world or Life or God.

Damaging those connections at any level creates separation, schism, isolation. One definition of insanity is disunity, isolation.

Does the fragmentation of modern industrial society explain skyrocketing domestic abuse and a sense of disconnection from reality? It does. But maybe the explanation, too, is the disintegration of whole ecosystems, or the millennium approaching.

I know a guy who feels himself ripped to pieces because his ex-wife demands that their son accept the "fact" that the kid's world is divided. There is no bridge except resentment. The poor guy keeps hoping that their boy will come to see that all worlds are interconnected, not schismatic, but that's not what the child's primary lesson seems to be.

I know a woman whose career is so consuming that she can think of nothing better than to quit to raise a garden and babies. But she can't quit because she's sacrificed too much to get to the professional point she's at, because if she left her known life, the fear of what could go wrong is paralyzing.

I'm impressed by how many hundreds of thousands of miles of new roads have been built in the United States in the last few generations—logging roads and mining roads and subdivision roads and National Park roads and eight-lane superhighways. They're all designed to bring us and everything closer together, to "open up" our lives.

But if our immediate lives remain constricted, guarded, divisive, then seeking connection anywhere Out There is useless. The fractures inside beg unity first.

To make any intimate relationship whole requires unconditional love. That's a tautology. It doesn't mean unconditional agreement or deference. It means love.

To save the children or the bears, to heal the planet or ourselves, a sense of wholeness has to grow from within, embracing progressively wider worlds.

Look at your intimate relationships now and in the past—with parents and children, friends and lovers, a special piece of music or fishing hole, deity or dream. When things were good, when there was real love and its union, could anything ever be better?

Now look around. Look for that connection. It's yours to choose. It's everywhere.

ᴧᴧᴧᴧ ULTIMATELY

I used to get angry at what seemed evil in my world. I'd rail at timber clear-cut proposals in the upper valley and at plans to blast new highways across the Alaska Range. I'd fulminate against engineering studies to construct a great hydro-electricity dam just above Talkeetna that would flood vast canyons.

When I realized, by coming out of the woods to talk with the "visionaries" who advanced those ideas, that those people were just like the rest of us, trying to do something that seemed important—even *good*—I sunk into despair.

They might devastate the valley, but they slept well at night, and woke exhilarated to keep working intently toward their dreams. And lots of decent people supported them.

Now I try to walk the line between helpless fury and helpless resignation.

Insistent desire for *results* is what's gotten our civilization what it now has, which includes the capacity for nuclear, climatic, and environmental annihilation. My original hope in moving remote to escape economic and cultural and personal struggle is no different than any other hope to busily "fix" what seems lacking. *Wanting* overlooks what sustenance already exists.

There's little chance to alter any destiny, even our own lives, except by first understanding what already is here, there, anywhere.

In Aboriginal Australia human beings have lived continuously as a single people for forty thousand years. Human beings didn't even know that North America and South America *existed* until, at the furthest extreme, 35,000 years ago. The Australian Aboriginal culture and worldview maintained itself for all of the time when Neanderthal cave men struggled against Cro-Magnon cave men to become us—European and Navajo and Chinese and Ethiopian. The longest-lived humans know what exists in their land, but they are baffled by and dying from the recent intrusion of colonization, which has altered profoundly what they've always known.

In aboriginal Alaska, the Eskimos—the Yupik and Inupiaq people—maintained a culture and worldview for thousands of years, but they, too, are unable to understand the extent to which their world is being changed. They, too, like the original Australians, turn to the land for sustenance but then turn their gaze outward in shock, in rage or resignation. Understanding the world is not simply a function of place anymore, though that's where it begins and ultimately ends if the conception of place is expansive enough.

To truly *see* the world in which we live can only result in stillness, stopped in one's tracks, staggered and humbled by how much is right underfoot, overhead, within grasp, complex beyond immediate comprehension but awaiting vision.

I no longer insist on an agenda for what this valley should become, though I ache for what might die from capitulation to mindless human greed. It's hard enough just seeing what this valley is, truly seeing the patterns (or lack of pattern) of climate and big game and human evolution, the cycles of ice sheets and morality, the mysterious behaviors of ravens in winter and people in town, the secrets of wilderness and the magic of light.

There's miracle here that's evident in the land and there's revelation that's startling in our response. It waits to be recognized for what it reveals both about us and that which exists beyond us.

We might not get it. But it's here, still.